JOHN DEERE
Two-Cylinder Tractor
BUYER'S GUIDE

John Dietz

Voyageur Press

First published in 2006 by MBI Publishing Company LLC
and Voyageur Press, an imprint of MBI Publishing Company,
Galtier Plaza, Suite 200, 380 Jackson Street, St. Paul, MN
55101-3885 USA

The information in this book is true and complete to the best
of our knowledge. All recommendations are made without any
guarantee on the part of the author or Publisher, who also
disclaim any liability incurred in connection with the use of
this data or specific details.

This publication has not been prepared, approved, or licensed
by John Deere.

We recognize, further, that some words, model names, and
designations mentioned herein are the property of the
trademark holder. We use them for identification purposes
only. This is not an official publication.

MBI Publishing Company titles are also available at discounts
in bulk quantity for industrial or sales-promotional use. For
details write to Special Sales Manager at MBI Publishing
Company, Galtier Plaza, Suite 200, 380 Jackson Street,
St. Paul, MN 55101-3885 USA

Library of Congress Cataloging-in-Publication Data

Dietz, John, 1946-
  John Deere two-cylinder buyer's guide / John Dietz.
      p. cm.
  ISBN-13: 978-0-7603-2445-5 (softbound)
  ISBN-10: 0-7603-2445-X (softbound)
  1. John Deere tractors—Purchasing. 2. John Deere tractors—
History. I. Title. II. Title: John Deere two-cylinder buyer's guide.
  TL233.6.J64D54 2006
  629.225'2—dc22
                                        2006017646

Editor: Amy Glaser
Designer: Christopher Fayers

Printed in China

Credits:
On the cover:
A 730 diesel. John Dietz

On the back cover:
Top:
The Waterloo Boy Model N, the final variation in the Waterloo
Boy series, was made between 1917 and 1924. This is a
1920 edition in Minnesota. Doug Easterlund
Bottom:
A porthole provides access to the starter and electrical
connections. Electric starting was new and optional when this
tractor was built. Dale Ridenour

Contents

Introduction

The John Deere two-cylinder tractor stands as an icon of modern farming. It represents the transition from animal power to machine power, from all farming prior to the twentieth century to twenty-first century agriculture. There were other important lines of tractors, perhaps equally important in fact, but the pre-1960s green or green-and-yellow Deere has a unique place. This book will update collectors, enthusiasts, and would-be collectors as to the current markets for these tractors. This book updates a 160-page book with the same title, published in 1992 and written by Robert N. Pripps.

Fourteen years after the initial buyer's guide things have changed. Thanks to the collaboration of Deere & Company with Two Cylinder Club, the production records between Waterloo Boy and 1960 have been carefully combed and organized for collectors. Today, the exact production numbers are known and published for nearly every version of a Deere two-cylinder tractor, whether common or rare, that came out of the factories in Iowa and Illinois. That production information is foundational for buyers, collectors, and anyone writing about Deere's two-cylinder tractors. It is available in much more detailed publications directly from the Two Cylinder Club. Several other books now contain those numbers, including this buyer's guide, but they were not available in 1992 at anything like the current level.

This book benefits from technology developments in the intervening years. One is the Internet, which has been essential in researching this guide and can be used by readers who want to update information found here. Using the search functions, it is possible to spend hundreds of hours on the Internet learning about these tractors and the entire industry that has developed in support of tractor hobbyists. For instance, a parts price list is one of the new features of this guide. It represents a range of parts prices posted on the Internet at about 20 separate sites, as of early 2006, and without distinction as to source or quality. Prices are constantly changing, but the prices in this book will give you an idea of the cost. If you look hard on the Internet, suppliers can be found for most of the parts needed for most of the two cylinder tractors. Similarly, the Internet is a gateway to collector discussion groups, collector clubs, major collector events, restoration people, publications, and more.

A major contribution has been made by Greg Peterson's database, known as www.machinerypete.com. Peterson has a monthly column in *Successful Farming* magazine. Machinery Pete is the primary source of price trend charts and current tractor value statements by the author. The company has been compiling auction sale price data on all types of farm and construction equipment throughout the United States since 1989. It works with more than 700 regional auctioneers to compile this data. The databases also reflect equipment available for sale on upcoming auctions and equipment available through implement dealers. Auction value trend charts produced from this data accurately show the trend of average sales for a specific model in each year indicated, within limits. Regional differences exist and are not indicated. Average sales value in a given year may be highly skewed if only two or three exceptional tractors were sold. From the master lists of sales for individual models, some extremely high value sales have been removed; some extremely low values (less than $500 or sales for parts) have been removed.

It is estimated that more than 50,000 readers worldwide subscribe to either of two glossy magazines devoted to John Deere's early farm tractors and supporting implements: *Green Magazine* and *Two Cylinder Club*. Both are highly recommended. Each publisher has produced numerous publications which are essential, in one way or another, for anyone who wants serious knowledge about the two cylinder tractor.

In the course of a year or research and writing on this subject, I learned that this is a passionate industry. A hobbyist

This is a rare Model 320 Special which is also known as the 320V. It has a standard tread and the slant steering wheel. *Bruce Keller*

can invest 500 shop hours, plus cash, to restore just one beloved old tractor. Completing a ground-up restoration is a serious accomplishment, a huge challenge in its own way equal to a marathon run or climbing a mountain. The common interest draws hobbyists together at national and statewide events, in clubs and coffee shops, and online chats. Specialists support the hobbyists, devoting entire careers to serving the hobbyists' interests. With their help, the icon of early twentieth century farming continues to putt-putt in thousands of private collections.

Approximately 150 individuals were contacted personally in the research for this work. Among them, special thanks to Restoration Advisors: Alan Jarosz, Albert Ulrich, Charles Lindstrom, Cork Groth, Dan Steiner, Don Sharp, Gary Uken, Gene Tencza, Glen Parker, Greg Stephen, Harvey Hamilton, John Shephard, Junior Roberts, Ken Kass, Kenny Earman, Larry Baker, Malcolm McIntyre, Ron Jungmeyer, Steve Ridenour, Terry Robison, and Travis Jorde. Special thanks for photos and extra effort with photography to: Bruce Keller, Dale Ridenour, Dave Hadam, Dixon Somerville, Eddie Campbell, Elmer Friesen, Jacob Merriwether, John Detmer, Ken Arundell, Kenny Earman, Leon Rumpf, Ron Jungmeyer, Doug Easterlund, Gerry Dubrick, and Steve Kidd.

Special thanks to my family for encouraging me to go ahead with this first book project; and to the true Great Collector/Restoration Expert for enabling me to complete it.

A Waterloo Boy Model R at the Manitoba Agricultural Museum in Austin, Manitoba. Note the chain steering and low fuel tank.
John Dietz

Chapter 1

Waterloo Boy

Birthplaces. As a lawyer traces the roots of his profession to ancient Athens and as a statesman traces his roots to Rome, many modern farmers trace their roots to Dixon, Illinois, and Waterloo, Iowa. This writer traces his own roots to Waterloo, where his mother was born at the end of June 1915.

The world's first commercially successful, self-scouring steel plow was born on a forge in John Deere's blacksmith shop in the village of Grand Detour (Dixon), Illinois, in 1837. Deere & Company's first commercially successful two-cylinder farm tractor was born in the Waterloo Traction Works Company in Waterloo, Iowa, in 1914. Four years later, Deere & Co. purchased the Waterloo factory, enabling Deere to become a full-line supplier of agricultural machinery.

The birthing process for the four-wheel, rear-wheel-drive Waterloo Boy tractor began in the Dakotas in 1892. The success of steam engines for threshing power had stimulated interest in a traction machine that could replace horses for cultivating and seeding. It had to be much lighter than the huge steam engines and affordable for an individual farm. The process of converting concept to workable machine took engineers, inventors, and factories the better part of 20 years.

The Waterloo factory had a successful two-cylinder stationary gasoline engine by 1911 and put some research into its own kerosene-fueled, portable version of the Waterloo Boy. It went through several design variations in rapid succession. Waterloo placed its first serial numbers, 1000 and 1001, on the L design in early 1914. A slightly revised design, called the LA, was even better and went into limited production for a few months. Waterloo produced 29 of these LA tractors in two styles in the first half of 1914; one style had four wheels and the other had three wheels. Some sold, but today none is known to exist from among these earliest models of the Waterloo Boy.

A more powerful two-cylinder engine was nearly ready in June 1914. This time the design worked and the Waterloo Boy R rolled into the history books. Although designed and built by the Traction Works, this machine would be known later as Deere's first commercially successful tractor. The basic two-cylinder, four-cycle horizontal engine with overhead valves was common to the design of all Waterloo-built tractors for the next 46 years. When the two-cylinder-farm-tractor era ended in 1960, the Waterloo factory had turned out approximately 1.3 million two-cylinder tractors. Today John Deere Waterloo Operations continues to specialize in tractor engine research and manufacture. It is said to be the world's oldest tractor factory.

Waterloo, however, would not be the only Deere two-cylinder tractor factory. When it made the Waterloo purchase in 1918, Deere & Co. already had a successful farm implement manufacturing business at Moline, Illinois. In time, Moline became world headquarters for Deere. The Waterloo factory was 140 miles northwest of Moline. In 1936, Deere began building a series of smaller two-cylinder tractors in space available at its Wagon Works factory in Moline. Over a 10-year production period, Deere workers built approximately 30,000 tractors at Moline. Finally, in 1947, Deere built an entirely new tractor factory at Dubuque, Iowa, 75 miles north of Moline. Dubuque built midsize tractors powered by engines with a vertical cylinder orientation, as opposed to the horizontal engines built at Waterloo. Dubuque built about 230,000 tractors between 1947 and 1960.

What is the value of any surviving automobile that first rolled off Henry Ford's new assembly line in Detroit? Hard to say. It's like asking what's the value of a Gutenberg Bible? Words like "value" and "collectable" really don't apply. Holding title to a Waterloo Boy isn't about collecting or dollar value or ownership, it's about history and about civilization. Happily, a few hundred Waterloo Boy tractors still exist. There are rumors of another one, somewhere, but if any Waterloo Boy tractor has been truly discovered in the past 10 to 15 years, it is a well-kept secret. The nearly completely disassembled, heavily rusted and worn remains of a Waterloo Boy on a northern Great Plains farm fetched more than $30,000 at auction in 2002 because of what it represented and because it could be restored. For collectors, even the serial number identification plate for one of these original tractors is particularly valuable.

Model R

The surviving cornerstone of today's tractor production, worldwide, is the Waterloo Boy R. The number known to exist is between 50 and 100, which is less than 1 percent of production. The Model R wasn't really the first tractor from the Waterloo Gasoline Engine Company, but it was the first tractor anywhere that went into full-scale commercial production. The first Model R was shipped on August 8, 1914. By December 15, 1915, it appears that 46 had been built. The last recorded shipping date was December 18, 1918. Between those dates, Waterloo built approximately 9,300 Model R Waterloo Boy tractors.

The Waterloo Boy R represented a breakthrough in technology. It was very reliable compared to other early tractors. It was easy to operate, rugged, priced right, and burned kerosene for fuel. The new two-cylinder engine design had a 180-degree firing order, producing an engine that was

A 1917 Waterloo Boy Model R. *Doug Easterlund*

smooth, powerful, and compact. Kerosene was abundant and inexpensive at the time. The Model R was initially priced at $750. The tractor had enough power to handle three 14-inch plows in most conditions, although it was rated officially for two plows. It had a simple gearbox with a choice of either forward or reverse. Flying forward at 2½ miles per hour, it could leave plowing horse teams in the dust.

The original engine block was bored to 5½ inches for each cylinder. The pistons had a 6-inch stroke. Bore was increased twice to give the engine even more power. The bore was 6 inches for R engines in 1915 and 1916. Engines after 1917 were bored to 6.5 inches. Piston stroke stayed a constant 7 inches. Rated rpm also increased from 700 to 750 in the later two engines. This third-generation Waterloo Boy R engine had a 465-ci capacity. It wasn't fast, but it had power. The Waterloo Boy R tipped the scale at more than 5,300 pounds of steel, iron, brass, aluminum, copper, tin, and glass. With steel wheels on loose soil the R still could pull two or three 14-inch plows tirelessly and faithfully.

From the start, Waterloo's assembly lines were always improving the product. Generations of change in engine design were not unique to the Waterloo Boy. The R went through many other design developments in its short production cycle, and virtually every model that followed at Waterloo, Moline, and Dubuque also would be modified many times during the production cycle.

However, the R may have been the most modified or revised tractor in history. Twelve major changes are recorded in 40 months of shipments. Waterloo designated each change with a second letter after the R, going alphabetically from A through M. Most changes are associated with valves and magnetos.

For instance, Waterloo built 39 three-wheel, or tricycle, versions of its tractor for work in orchards and vegetable crops on the West Coast between December 15, 1914 and August 31, 1917. Known as the California Special[1], none of these three-wheel tractors is known to exist today. Within the group, according to Two-Cylinder® Club historian J. R. Hobbs, there were variations. Differences include one or two front wheels, an optional integral two-bottom plow, and even a more maneuverable short-wheelbase version. One was apparently exported to Panama.

A one-speed transmission lever—forward or reverse—that is located beside the gasoline supply is used for starting the engine. *Doug Easterlund*

During 1914 to 1919, while World War I was raging in Europe, the American farm economy was relatively prosperous. Demand increased for exported farm products, including the new tractors. In Britain, farmers were looking for a traction machine that could replace teams of horses. Waterloo Boy R fit the niche once they were discovered. During the war years, Deere exported about 4,000 Waterloo Boy tractors to Britain. They were renamed and repainted there and were sold as "Overtime" tractors for the farms of England and Ireland. Destinations also included France, Greece, Denmark, and South Africa.

Within a few years, the Waterloo Boy Rs were working in most farming areas of North America. Their active era on farms lasted into the 1930s. It wasn't long before there were better, more powerful tractors coming off assembly lines at high production rates. During World War II, there was a huge demand for iron, copper, and other metals to support the war effort. By 1945, most Waterloo Boys had gone the way of scrap metal and were recycled into material for war supplies.

A Word to Collectors

Waterloo Gasoline Engine Company had made stationary two-cylinder Waterloo Boy engines for several years before introducing the Waterloo Boy R. Most stationary engines had two flywheels, but some had only one flywheel and were very similar to the tractor engine with its single flywheel. In the records, some serial numbers of stationary engines and engines for tractors are intermixed. This has led to some mix-ups for modern collectors.

Anyone interested in the restoration of any tractor will need access to production information specific to that model's place in the production cycle, as determined by the serial number. The serial number can be used to find the manufacturing date, shipping date, destination point, and other notes about the specific tractor. Unofficial information on serial numbers and related information is available from numerous sources, including publications, clubs, dealers, and Internet sites.

Official records for all Waterloo Boy and later two-cylinder John Deere tractors now are available through the Two-Cylinder®

Club, a collectors' organization based in the Iowa villages of Grundy Center and Reinbeck, about 25 miles southwest of Waterloo. The Two-Cylinder® Club is a nonprofit service, educational, and recreational organization. It extends an invitation of membership to anyone interested in the preservation of John Deere tractors and implements and their important role in our agricultural heritage.

Waterloo Boy N

The first Waterloo Boy N was shipped on January 3, 1918, just two weeks after the last R was shipped. The initial price was $1,050. The last N was shipped on October 15, 1924. Records indicate that approximately 20,500 Waterloo Boy N tractors were built, which is equal to about 100 for each working day

at Waterloo. No one knows how many survive today, but a fair estimate seems to be about 1 percent. Market value for a fully restored N now may be 100 times the original purchase price.

Deere & Co. purchased the Waterloo Gasoline Engine Company for $2,350,000 on March 14, 1918. Deere had invested nearly a quarter million dollars in its own tractor research since 1912 and had a workable three-wheel-drive tractor by 1917. However, after careful investigation, directors decided it was better to purchase the already successful Waterloo facility than risk further pursuit of its own four-cylinder, three-wheel design.

The distinctly different feature of an N when compared to an R was the enclosed two-speed transmission. It could move in high gear at about 3 miles per hour and gave the

Detail of the Model N auto-steer system. The Model N came with either the chain steering system or this early rack-and-pinion type of steering. *Doug Easterlund*

The Model N drive gear is full size and located under the rear-wheel rim. Be sure all the teeth are still present and firmly attached. This is a 1922 model in Washington. *Ken Langel*

operator more flexibility in tackling field chores. Deere continued to use the 365-ci engine, first used on the R, throughout the production cycle of the N.

Improvements continued as Waterloo Boy Ns rolled off the line. Engineers soon developed a larger radiator for the N. In March 1919 the fuel tank was raised 3 inches with a longer bracket, and it was raised another 3 inches in June 1919. The serial number plate and crankshaft counterweight were moved. The fan and water pump were combined into a single unit. Different sets of decals for the N were designed and the painting scheme was revised in January 1920. From then on, the N was to be John Deere green except for red hubcaps and highly selective uses of red and yellow at other strategic points.

In February 1920, Deere changed the steering system. The N and R had used a roller and heavy chains to pivot the front axle. As chains and rollers wore down, it took more turns of the steering wheel to turn the tractor. Deere replaced the chain system with a steering system similar to one that was being used on automobiles and called it auto-steer.

A Waterloo Boy N with auto-steer made history for another reason in the spring of 1920. It was the first tractor tested under a new tractor-testing law in Nebraska. Nebraska Tractor Tests became the industry standard for rating and comparing tractors. Nebraska Test No. 1 was taken on March 31, 1920, on the Waterloo Boy N.

In August and September 1920, Waterloo equipped 24 N tractors with a special air filtering system (the clarifier) for dusty field conditions. The 24 California Clarifier[2] tractors went to the rapidly growing commercial vegetable industry in California and Oregon, as had the previous California Special. It was thought that none of the clarifiers had survived, until one

Model N production in 1919 used a chain for the fan and water pump drive on this tractor, serial number 16173. *Doug Easterlund*

The same fan and water pump system used a simpler belt drive and only green paint months later on serial number 27539. *Doug Easterlund*

This is the driver's station on the Model N. Note the offset steering. *Doug Easterlund*

was discovered by accident in 1998. Richard Wheeler, a Washington state resident, purchased a Waterloo Boy N in Idaho with what appeared to be an odd piece attached to the tractor. The odd piece was later identified as the clarifier, still attached to the original tractor, and is the only one known to exist.

One further change to note was implemented on September 30, 1920. From serial number 28094 onwards to the end of production, the Waterloo Boy had a riveted frame rather than a bolted frame.

This one-of-a-kind California Clarifier is bolted to the wooden deck of Dick Wheeler's Model N in Washington. *Richard Wheeler*

Waterloo Boy Anecdotes:

"We have a 1924 Waterloo Boy N. My dad and I bought it in 1972. We paid $750 for it. It was in very good condition. The guy had restored it to the point where it ran and he painted it. We've never done anything to it except maintained [it] over the years. He was a former John Deere dealer whose interests had turned toward horses. We do drive it occasionally, put it in parades. I know my clutch isn't very good, so it's probably 15 years since we plowed with it."

—Doug Easterlund, St. Cloud, Minnesota

"I grew up in Wisconsin. While I was going to high school, on weekends I used to drive a milk truck for my dad and we used to pick [up] the milk from a farmer that had this 1922 Waterloo Boy tractor. In 1947, people weren't interested in that stuff. . . . It's in pretty decent shape today in my shop. To my knowledge, that engine's never been touched and that thing runs just perfect. We have all the documentation on this tractor. The serial number on the brass tag [matches in the company record with] the one on the magneto base, one on the engine housing, and one on the transmission."

—Ken Langel, Lynden, Washington

"I got my Waterloo Boy N in January 1966. There wasn't a bolt in it. It was [all] just in a pile. . . . I asked Neil what he wanted for it. He said $200. I said I'll give you $175 for it and I'll take home parts of it now, and in the spring come to get the rest. The rest is history. My father was a former JD dealer and mechanic. He had worked for the dealership when they were popular. We [Dad and I] did get it together and had it running in two years."

—Doug Holcomb, Eau Claire, Wisconsin

"I've redone about 90 Waterloo Boys and I usually have one or two in my shop. Usually you need new wrist pins, bushings, rod bearings, and main bearings when you go to rebuild the engine. I make new fans, pulleys, shafts, bearings, and other parts. Anything that was made once can be made again."

—Ken Kass, Dunkerton, Iowa

Collectors' Notes

Availability

It is possible, but highly unlikely, that any discarded, unclaimed Waterloo Boy tractors still exist. All known units are in private collections, owned by clubs, or in museum-type collections. Typically they are highly treasured and not available at any price. Demand is so high that when one is sold, it is likely to command 100 times the original market price or more.

Value

"I was at an auction in September 2004 in western Minnesota. There was a Waterloo Boy N at that auction. It had sat outside for at least 15 years. It was unbelievable, how bad it was, and that tractor sold for $33,000." —Doug Easterlund, St. Cloud, Minnesota

"If I had to buy one of those things [a Waterloo Boy that's running], it would be something in excess of $50,000." — Ken Langel, Lynden, Washington

"Value will range anywhere from $50,000 to $80,000 for a Waterloo Boy tractor, depending on condition. We've got about 300 in North America, but you've got a lot of John Deere collectors and that's the foundation."—Ken Kass, Dunkerton, Iowa

Restoration/Watch Out

1. If the tractor isn't working, don't assume the engine has its pistons or that the gearbox has its gears. The seller may not even be aware they're missing!
2. Watch out for heavily worn drive gears on the main wheels. This is a cast-on-cast system.
3. A first glance can be deceiving. A few Waterloo Boys have been patched together from a mix of parts and pieces that don't match.
4. Radiators and kerosene tanks always need to be replaced on unrestored Waterloo Boys. Don't even hope to find a used one; plan to have it custom made.

The Waterloo Boy Model N, the final variation in the Waterloo Boy series, was made between 1917 and 1924. This is a 1920 edition in Minnesota. *Doug Easterlund*

5. Modern replacement bearings won't fit a Waterloo Boy. Plan to hire a machinist to build bearings and whatever holds them in place.
6. Painting schemes and the right shades of paint are available for the Waterloo Boy, but doing a good job of painting will require a lot of disassembly work first.
7. It's very hard to replace the brass carburetor bowl or the glass oil pressure bottle for a Waterloo Boy. Easy replacement items include the magneto, drive belts, radiator fan, and seat.

Waterloo Boy Specifications

Model	L/LA	R	N
Years produced	1913–1914	1914–1919	1917–1924
First serial number (1914)	1000	1026	10000
Last serial number	1253	10336	31412
Total built	29	9,310	21,392
Price (new)	--	$850	$1,050
Drawbar horsepower	7	12	12
PTO/belt horsepower	15	25	25
Forward/reverse speeds	1/1	1/1	2/1
Weight (lb)	3,000	5,420	5,930
Wheelbase length (in)	142	143	132
Height to radiator (in)	63	63	63
Width (in)	72	71	
Front steel wheels (in)	28x6	28x6	28x6
Rear steel wheels (in)	52x10	52x10	52x12
Fuel capacity (gal)	--	20	20
Coolant capacity (qt)	--	34	34
Nebraska Test No.	--	--	1
Test date	31/03/1920		
Maximum pull (lb)		2,900	
Plows (14 in)		3	

Engine	1913–1914	1914–1915	1915–1917	1917–1924	1917–1918
Fuel	Kerosene	Kerosene	Kerosene	Kerosene	Kerosene
Bore and stroke (in)	5.5x7.00	5.5x7.00	6.00x7.00	6.5x7.00	6.50x7.00
Displacement (ci)	333	330	396	465	465
Maximum rpm	700	700	750	750	750

Part	Availability [Yes/No/Custom]		
		Manifold	Custom
		Oil gauge bottle	No
		Paint	Yes
Axle roller bearings	Custom	Piston	Custom
Bushings	Custom	Piston rods	Custom
Carburetor parts	Some	Piston rod bearings	Custom
Clutch lining	Yes	Radiator fan	Custom
Clutch casting	Custom	Radiator shroud	Custom
Clutch parts	Custom	Seat	Yes
Connecting rod	Custom	Seat brackets	Custom
Crankcase oil breather	Custom	Starting crank	Custom
Crankshaft	Custom	Steering chain	Yes
Crankshaft bearings	Custom	Steering chain gear	Custom
Decals	Yes	Steering chain roller bearing	Custom
Drive belt	Yes	Throttle lever	Custom
Engine block	No	Transmission	No
Fender	Custom	Transmission shaft	Custom
Flywheel	Custom	Water pump	Custom
Kerosene tank	No	Wheels, front	No
Magneto	Yes	Wheels, rear	Yes
Main bearing	Custom	Wheel lugs	Custom

Reported Sale Prices*

Model R	1919	England	1-27-2001	$20,000
	?	North Carolina	6-2002	$54,000
Model N	1920	Wisconsin	6-12-2004	$39,000
	?	North Carolina	6-2002	$34,000
	?	South Dakota	6-2003	$32,000
	?	Illinois	7-2002	$52,000

*Various sources, not verified

Showroom tractors deserve a showroom. An early Model D (left) on steel is one highlight in this southwest Ontario private showroom built by collectors Steve Kidd and Robert Kraehling. *Gerry Dubrick*

Chapter 2

Models D, R, 80, 820, 830

Tractors in the 1920s were perhaps as revolutionary in their time as desktop computers were in 1980s offices. Buyers were replacing teams of horses; they had just become comfortable with automobiles and trucks. In 1923, Deere replaced the Waterloo Boy with the Model D tractor, which was a big step forward in technology. It didn't take long for the Model D to become hugely successful. Other assembly lines with other types of tractors started gearing up at Waterloo soon after 1923, but the Model D stayed in production for many years. In the 1940s, a second, similar family of tractors was launched at Waterloo. This was the Model R family that was powered by diesel fuel as opposed to the kerosene used in Model D tractors.

Both families were large tractors, mainly suited to midsize and larger Midwestern farms. They relied on a low center of gravity, sheer weight from lots of iron, and the sturdy two-cylinder engine for tremendous pulling power. Several wheel types were offered, but the basic tractor had only one configuration.

Other family lines from Waterloo were quite different. They were generally known as row-crop tractors. They were more agile, steered better, and often were purpose-built for production applications. They were offered in three to six configurations. Most had a choice of engines powered by kerosene, gasoline, diesel, or all-fuel.

Both Model D and Model R tractor families were built with what became known as the standard tread front-axle design. They were built like a steerable, self-propelled farm wagon. Front wheel tread was as wide as the rear tread. On the Waterloo Boy, the front axle had pivoted. On these tractors, the front axle was stationary. Designers equipped the tractor with a set of running gears used on automobiles and steam engines to turn the wheels rather than pivoting the entire axle. When new configurations were introduced on row-crop tractors, this straight, beam-axle design became known as standard tread.

Deere built approximately 160,000 Model D tractors over a manufacturing life of 30 years. The model was so successful and basic that Deere kept building it for more years than any other model of tractor that Deere has ever produced (the production life of many tractor models is less than five years). However, the basic Model D went through a continuous series of revisions. These upgrades give it great diversity. Collectors can specialize in the Model D and have quite a large collection.

The Model R family went through four name changes after its 1949 introduction. For 1955, soon after the Model D was phased out, the R was renamed the Model 80. It became the 820 in 1956 and the 830 in 1958. These were large, powerful diesel fuel tractors. Most were started with a gasoline-fired, four-cylinder engine. Recently they have become a popular big-power tractor at tractor pulling competitions. The series of big diesels was manufactured for 12 years and approximately 39,000 were sold.

Model D

The Model D is "the tractor that set the standard for ALL John Deere tractors" according to the 1937 pamphlet marking the 100th anniversary of Deere & Company. It was true then, and it still is. The Model D was an instant success in the early years. It sold itself on the basis of performance in the field, economy, simplicity, and accessibility. If you had a farm in the Midwest, the Model D was a very good option. It was a heavy-duty tractor, built to pull a three-bottom plow or other implements on big, wide-open fields. It could also operate a belt

The Nickel Hole D earned its name from the nickel-size hole at each end of the slot on the solid flywheel. *Bruce Keller*

for other farm jobs. Sales were strong for most of its production life except for the middle of the Great Depression, World War II, and the early 1950s.

Today it is still reasonably easy to find a member of the Model D family with a "for sale" sign on it in the region where they were popular more than 50 years ago. They stood up well, and many were restored along the way. Many that were parked in fence rows and empty buildings in the 1970s and later have been found and salvaged by the current generation of collectors.

Whether it's the right machine for the collector is a different story. The D is a big tractor. It requires a heavy-duty trailer for transport and is not easy to work on in a small shop. On the other hand, it is relatively simple in design. Deere engineers saved their rocket science for models that were introduced in the 1950s as the two-cylinder era was closing. Deere dealers today still can supply many parts for Model D tractors, or usually they can find them through various parts networks.

Some of the most prized antique tractors in the world today are found in the Model D family. A few are so rare and prized that a six-figure purchase offer won't shake them loose from the proud owners. However, many other valued but more common Model D tractors are available and being collected. They are fairly easy to find in the right part of the continent. For a farm shop, it can be a good introductory project without a major cash investment.

A watershed in the two-cylinder era needs to be mentioned at this point. Deere decided it was time to put a modern face on their product as North America and Europe came out of the Great Depression. Like automobiles, washing machines, and toasters, the product had matured. By the late 1930s, the market wanted style, as well as form and function. Starting in 1939, over a period of about three years, all of the Deere assembly lines at Waterloo began building styled tractors.

Styled D production began on April 7, 1939, with serial number 143800. That tractor was shipped to Calgary, Alberta. Historians estimate that about 50,000 styled D farm tractors were shipped to western Canada. Any tractor built before the advent of styled tractors in that line became known as the unstyled version. In 1939, approximately 110,000 Model D tractors built before the styling watershed became known as unstyled D tractors. The same fate occurred as Deere's row-crop tractor families became styled. Today collectors sometimes specialize in styled or unstyled tractor collections.

Within the Model D family, there are early, mid, and late unstyled D tractors. Any early unstyled Model D is to be prized. Waterloo manufactured 23,000 units in this run from 1923 through 1927. The mid D series began with the 1928 model year. Horsepower was boosted by increasing the cylinder bore a half-inch to 6¾ inches. The mid D now had slightly more than 28 horsepower on the drawbar and 36 horsepower on the belt when tested at Nebraska. In just three production years, Deere built 56,000 of these tractors. The late unstyled D was introduced for 1931. Engine bore and stroke stayed the same, but the engine was all new from the crankshaft forward. The late D series ran for nine model years, through 1939, with a total production of 33,000 units.

The early D came standard for $1,112 with 4-inch lugs on the four steel wheels, a swing drawbar, operator's platform, and fenders. Popular options included a $3 muffler, $1 steering wheel handle, $2 radiator curtain, 6-inch rear-wheel extension rims for $31, and a power shaft assembly for $38. The mid D basic price, with a power shaft assembly, increased to $1,119. A late D price list offers the basic tractor with huge 5-inch spade lugs on the steel wheels for $1,125. The spoke wheel option for new pneumatic tires increased the base price to $1,400.

Mid and late Model D tractors had many options. Trying to find them all today is one of the joys (or challenges) for modern collectors. Wheel options are one example. It appears that the first Deere tractor equipped with rubber tires for agricultural use was a late unstyled D that was shipped in August

This 1926 Model D in Manitoba has the large spade lugs, which are ideal for grip in deep prairie soil. This flywheel had larger slot holes, making it easier to put on and remove. *Ken Arundell*

This original 1930 Model D on steel with front and rear spokes is ready for restoration. *John Detmer*

1933. The 1935 Model D was the first in commercial production to offer a three-speed transmission, as well as several other changes. Late in the same year, engineers solved some issues with the 6-spline rear axles by introducing new 12-spline axles. Changes and options for the Model D wheels kept coming. By the end of the late D unstyled series in 1939, there were options for steel wheels or rubber tires on either end of the tractor; a variety of lugs, scrapers, and extensions for steel-wheeled tractors; a few sets of skeleton rear wheels, which are reversible rear wheels that narrowed the tread to 47 inches for row-crops; and more. Here's a sampling of other options, if you have a mid or late D:

Mid D Options

Muffler and spark arrester
Auxiliary air cleaner
Exhaust elbow, Spark arrester
Drive wheel scrapers, Extension rim scrapers
Radiator guard, Drawbar shifter for sidehills
Electric lighting equipment, Citrus grove fenders
Speed reducer

Late D Options

Electric lighting, Bosch magnetos
Hot manifold routing exhaust to the right side of the tractor
Reversible rear wheels for row-crops
Radiator shutters controlled on-the-go
Short front axle for row-crops
28x6 angled flat-spoke front steel wheels
24x5 round-spoke front steel wheels
Cast disc front steel wheels for orchard service
Round-spoke front wheels for rubber tires

Spoker D

Among all two-cylinder tractors, the John Deere Spoker D stands at a near-legendary level for collectors. The status comes from the fact that these were the first true John Deere–designed tractors in successful commercial production. Fifty were manufactured in late 1923, followed by roughly 760 in 1924 and 2,000 in 1925. In December 1925, the original spoked flywheel was replaced with a solid flywheel. The initial series then became known as Spoker D tractors.

This 1930 Model D in Kansas, after restoration, has rubber boots to protect the paint and pavement.
John Detmer

This styled D on rubber was built in 1945. The styled treatment for the Model D was introduced in 1938. This has cast wheels for rubber, although all-steel was still an option.
Ken Arundell

A closer view of the engine and flywheel on this 1945 styled D. *Ken Arundell*

Among the Spoker D group, the first 50 are unique. They had ladder-style sides on the radiator, fabricated front axles, 26-inch spoked flywheels, steering wheels with four holes per spoke, and instructions stenciled on the rear of the fuel tank. Changes began with the 1924 production year. A one-piece malleable cast-iron front axle replaced the fabricated axle. The radiator had flat sides, the steering wheel had three spokes, and some lettering was changed. For 1925, the main case was revised so that Deere could offer its first power take-off (PTO). The flywheel diameter was reduced to 24 inches and the steering wheel now had two holes. The steering shaft was modified into a two-piece system that provided more space between the shaft and the flywheel.

Nickel Hole D

The solid flywheel was soon dubbed the Nickel Hole. It had a nickel-size hole at each end of the stress slot. It was better than the spoked flywheel, but problems soon developed. The stress slot was short and the relief hole was small. When wedges were driven into the stress slots to assemble the flywheel onto the crankshaft, it was prone to cracking. Deere modified the design and solved the problem in less than a year, but approximately 2,400 of the Nickel Hole D tractors had been sold. Deere launched a program to replace the nickel-hole flywheels with the later design; most were changed. As a result, the few that survive are among the biggest prizes that a Model D collector can find.

Corn Borer D

A third special member of the early unstyled Model D family is known as the Corn Borer Special. It was a standard Model D equipped with PTO and was originally purchased by the

Here is a closer view of the dash and steering wheel on this 1945 styled D. This one is equipped with battery, lights, and electric starter. *Ken Arundell*

The radiator decal on this 1945 D is correct. At least two companies specialize in decals for John Deere two-cylinder tractors. *Ken Arundell*

U.S. Department of Agriculture (USDA) in March or April 1927 for an equipment rental program. The program acquired 440 Model D and 360 Fordson tractors. The program was offered in New York, Pennsylvania, Ohio, Michigan, and Indiana, where farmers were still using teams of horses. For $1 an acre, farmers could park the horses, rent a tractor, a plow, and a PTO-driven "stubble beater." The purpose of the program was to help farmers combat the growing infestation of European corn borers by reducing or burying crop residue. The USDA identification numbers were stenciled on each tractor. Today they represent a particular era in the industry. They are hard to find, sometimes overlooked, and are highly prized by a few.

Experimental D

In July 1928, the first of two experimental Model D tractor designs rolled out of Waterloo. There were 100 serial number tags stamped with the letter *X* as a prefix for these experimental tractors known as the Exhibit A model. The experimental changes on these tractors worked very well in field conditions in 1929 and early 1930. Deere developed a few changes and selected a second set of 50 experimental tractors in July 1930. This time the serial number began with the

letter *B*. These are known as Exhibit B tractors. Most were shipped to Montana or Arizona. Ten tractors in the group were equipped with crawler tracks, which was Deere's first venture into that new market. One fully restored example of an Exhibit A tractor today is in the John Deere Tractor Museum near Wolf Point, Montana. This private collection, started by Louis Toavs, has more than 500 two-cylinder tractors and includes one or more Model D tractors for each production year.

The radiator decal on the 1926 unstyled D looks like the company was proud of its product. Note the filler holes for water, kerosene, and starter gasoline.
Ken Arundell

Depression D

The late unstyled Model D, incorporating most of the changes that had been tested on Exhibit A and Exhibit B units, was introduced in 1931. Sales were excellent. More than 5,600 were built for 1931. The model didn't change for 1932, but production nearly stopped due to the Great Depression and Dust Bowl conditions. Production of Model D tractors at Waterloo was very low in 1931 and 1932. Trying to find and restore one of these Depression-era Model Ds has become a special challenge for some collectors. There are various opinions on actual production numbers for 1932 and 1933. It seems that the total production in the two calendar years was no more than 804, and it may have been as low as 156 in 1932. They were identical to 1931 and 1934 higher production tractors and generate special interest. Any of these Depression D tractors that have been found in the past 20 years can be treasured.

War Years D

There were nine years of generally good sales after 1933. Model D production at Waterloo averaged about 4,100 tractors through the period. Wartime demands, however, diverted the supply of steel and other supplies. Model D production plunged in 1943 to just over 550 tractors. Production began to rebound in 1944 and hit a postwar peak in 1948 at more than 8,700 tractors. As a hard-to-find symbol of an era, the 1943 War Years D is a highly collectable tractor today even though the parts are the same on the higher-production 1942 or 1944 models.

Streeter D

The end of the 30-year Model D production run came on March 25, 1953, when the last recorded styled D rolled off the assembly line. However, that isn't the end of the Model D family. Spare parts were used later that year to build 92 additional styled Model D tractors with hand tools to meet a few last orders. The assembly point was a street location in Waterloo between a truck shop and a milling room. Tractors from this group, the Streeter D, are unique and highly prized because they were the last of a long line and because they were hand-built. Most of the Streeters were exported to Cuba, and some may still be there. Thirty-three were sent to work in Arkansas rice fields, and four were sent to dealers in Kansas, South Dakota, and Saskatchewan.

With 160,000 Model D tractors built over a period of 30 years, there are many thousands of surviving units in today's collector community. They come up at auction frequently. Machinery Pete has been tracking results of sales at rural equipment auctions since 1996. His observers have recorded more than 80 sales of Model D tractors between 1996 and 2005. Aumann Auctions, Inc., of Nokomis, Illinois, sold about 35 Model D tractors between April 2003 and December 2005. Aumann Auctions now has a searchable, public, online database of sales results covering several years.

Over the sales years and item-to-item, the recorded sales values have varied from a few hundred dollars for old iron value on a Model D to as much as $17,000 in 2005 for a restored Spoker D and $16,000 for a Streeter D from the other end of the production era. The trend chart that develops from selected sales indicates a nicely rising value for the Model D family. Values have perhaps doubled in 10 years. It is possible to purchase one in rough condition at auction for under $2,000, but $3,000 will buy a nice Model D in most places except for the real collector items.

Model D Buyers' Guide

"It's getting harder to find parts and pieces. When we got into it, the boom hadn't really taken off. We really started about 1986–87. There was quite a few around then. You also had to take some junkers, skeleton machines, so you could skaff off parts to make one that ran. Now you want them to be running if you're just getting one. That's definitely the way to go. Parts through John Deere have pretty well ceased. When we first got into it, they were selling [mufflers] for likely around sixty dollars. Now they're over two hundred. Same with rings and pistons." — Greg Campbell, Chater, Manitoba, Canada

"The original steel wheels, they're getting scarce now. If you do find one with steel and if it's sat in the mud, then the wheels are all pitted and that's bad. Carburetors, in the early ones, are brass and worn and everything's kind of loose. So,

Model R tractors were standard tread and diesel fueled. This is a nicely restored 1953 model on a working farm. *John Dietz*

This Model R starts with a big assist from a gas-fired pony engine that's under the hood. *John Dietz*

it'll rev up and idle down. Air cleaners are the biggest thing we've noticed. They were a real dinosaur with air. It would take a lot of dirt through, so a lot of guys added on oil bath breathers and threw away the original stuff. Now, trying to find the originals to put back on is a big thing." — Greg Campbell, Chater, Manitoba, Canada

"On a D, the only thing that's likely to be worn real bad is the engine. Unless they have parts available and a good machine shop and don't want to spend a lot of money, they need to find an engine that's free. As for the rest of a D, they're just so simple that you very seldom have a transmission problem that's anything other than maybe a bearing or a bushing. They're just an awful simple tractor." — Eugene Olson, Minden, Nebraska

"As you get into the older Ds, a lot of the parts were replaced with newer parts. They fit, but they're not proper for the tractor if you want the tractor really original. You get a good parts book and check the parts numbers. In the real early Ds, when they replaced the parts, Deere came along with an updated part that wasn't like the original but, in some cases, still carried the same part number. Even when the guys were farming with these tractors, they may have gone into the dealer for a part and have gotten a part with the same number, but

it still wasn't quite like the original—they were improved pieces." — Eugene Olson, Minden, Nebraska

"We mostly get calls for engine parts and cosmetic stuff on the D series; fenders, hood, and gas tank. Normal engine parts include carb, mag, a few cylinder heads. The transmission and rear end are real strong; seldom need repair. Good gas tanks are getting hard to keep [in stock]. Usually they have to repair the old tank if possible. If you get into the late Ds, the sheet metal, like front grilles, prices are terrible." — Junior Roberts, Steiner Tractor Parts, Flint, Michigan

"In them earlier ones, the lower shaft in the transmission seems to be worn out always. They've got a bushing in there instead of a bearing. It's a slow-turning shaft, but the ones I've seen are usually wore out." — Ron Jungmeyer, Jungmeyer Tractor Restoration Service, Russellville, Missouri

"Probably the hardest thing to work with, for repair, would be the early styled Splitdorf magnetos and early styled carburetors. Those carburetors sell for close to $1,000 because they're so hard to find. If you've got a Spoker D, you want to keep that thing pretty secure because the carburetor could get legs. Those old brass Splitdorf mags, the early ones, are really susceptible to moisture. They look nice and classy, but if you want to run that kind of stuff you need to make

This is serious tractor power. This two-cylinder diesel engine was rated for 45.7 horsepower on the drawbar in a tractor that weighed 10,400 pounds when shipped. *John Dietz*

sure you keep it in a dry area." — Albert Ulrich, Renaissance Tractor, Chehalis, Washington

"In the early 6.5-inch D era, blocks and heads, internals like pistons, etc., are getting extremely hard to find because there just aren't that many left. What's good out there is going to demand a price. If you're going to buy an early D that's a little bit of an Erector Set; you want to really make sure that

you've got a depth of parts to support it." — Albert Ulrich, Renaissance Tractor, Chehalis, Washington

"For working on, these [big] tractors are pretty straightforward. There isn't any rocket science in these. That's good for a collector, although the components are pretty heavy. The old D block is basically the frame of the tractor. Your front axle is attached to the bottom of the block. If you're going to do

A beautifully restored dash and correct decal in a Model R with electric start. *Ron Jungmeyer*

A 1953 Model 80. Note the teardrop-shaped flywheel cover and electric lights. The hood decal should read "JOHN DEERE," followed by "DIESEL" in italics. *John Dietz*

some block boring, you basically split the tractor in two when you take the block out." — Albert Ulrich, Renaissance Tractor, Chehalis, Washington

"Later Ds, for repairs, are pretty trouble-free. It's the typical freeze-crack stuff." — Albert Ulrich, Renaissance Tractor, Chehalis, Washington

" . . . some early Ds have warped intake manifolds. They won't run right if they warp enough to where the intake port

between the two exhaust ports on the intake manifold doesn't seal and will pull in some air." — Albert Ulrich, Renaissance Tractor, Chehalis, Washington

"One of the hardest things to work on those things, especially in the early styled D with a generator they drove off the fan shaft, is the fan shaft. You basically got to pull the whole fan shaft out to change the belt." — Albert Ulrich, Renaissance Tractor, Chehalis, Washington

This is a Model 80 from gopher-level on the passenger side. It was distinguished from the Model R by the flywheel cover and the words "JOHN DEERE" in small letters on the radiator. *John Dietz*

"A true spoked tractor will have a different internal hub in the wheels. Some guys will get down right to the spade configuration and count the spades on a wheel. Sometimes you find a real late styled D that has steel wheels may draw more attention than one that has rubber on it. Rubber was a standard feature and you had to order steel as an option." — Albert Ulrich, Renaissance Tractor, Chehalis, Washington

"Probably the hardest thing to find in a styled D is a good front grille. There's nobody making those in reproduction yet." — Albert Ulrich, Renaissance Tractor, Chehalis, Washington

"All the two-cylinders had a problem with getting water in the oil through head gaskets, cracked heads, and cracked blocks. If I'm buying one, I'll crack the drain plug on it to make sure I don't have that problem." — Larry Ott, Fergus Falls, Minnesota

Detail of the Model 80
engine, left side. *John Dietz*

The Model 80 had a
comfortable seat, power
steering, easy controls, and
360-degree visibility with
full fresh air. A few models
were built with a new all-
steel cab to protect the
operator. *John Dietz*

A Model 820, parked between parades, with an early all-steel cab. The 20 series tractors had bright yellow paint on the side panels, whereas the 80 and other first numbered series tractors were all green except for the wheels. *Jacob Merriwether*

Model R

A larger, more powerful, more versatile standard tread tractor than the Model D was commissioned in early 1940. The fuel was to be diesel. Diesel engines had proven to be more compact, powerful, and efficient than kerosene-driven engines. Diesel engines had excellent efficiency, power, torque curve, and low operating costs. They were difficult to start in cold weather due to higher fuel compression ratios.

After trials with a few experimental MX models, the Model R was rolling off Waterloo assembly lines in late 1947. The Model R was first introduced to dealers at Winnipeg, Manitoba, in June 1948. With 45 horsepower at the drawbar, the R could pull one more plow than the 38-horsepower Model D that it would replace. A little two-cylinder, gasoline-fired pup motor

started the big diesel engine. A magneto and electric starter for the gasoline engine simplified the start-up procedure.

This was the first time that Deere offered an all-steel tractor cab as an option. The R had other firsts for John Deere, such as an optional live PTO and live hydraulics controlled by a second clutch. The hydraulic circuit used the PTO for its source of power. A radiator shutter, hour meter, and wheel weights were optional. The series could be equipped with a wide variety of tires and wheels. It had options for 12- or 14-inch rear wheel rims, special tires, and mud shields for rice and sugarcane growers. Steel wheels could also be furnished for wet or extremely rough conditions.

The 1949 Model R production run amounted to about 1,420 tractors. Sales peaked at 5,800 units in 1952 and ended in 1954 with 3,200 units. By then, Deere was satisfied that it had a successful market entry with the big standard tread diesel. Engineers readied a set of upgrades while the company phased out its original standard tread, kerosene-fueled Model D. Deere abandoned letters in favor of numbers for naming tractor models. In 1955, the new tractors on the former Model R assembly lines were renamed as Model 80 tractors. Most Model R tractors had been sold to farmers in the wheat and small grain regions of the high plains and prairies. The production total shipped to the United States and Canada was 17,563. Another 3,570 were exported.

Trade in Model R tractors has been slow over the past 10 years, but the value of those being traded has shown a healthy and steady upward trend. A $2,300 Model R in 1996 was worth about $4,000 at the end of 2005. The highest recorded price at auction was $6,500 in 2000 for a 1952 Model R with new tires. The current average auction price in early 2006 seems to be about $3,700.

Model R Buyers' Guide

"The PTO gears usually are in highest demand. They shell the teeth off of them; they just wasn't strong enough. You've got to get out west more before you find much [parts for] the R, 80, 820, 830. There just wasn't many in this area. If your R needed something, I'd probably try to locate it for you on the Hotline." — Junior Roberts, Steiner Tractor Parts, Flint, Michigan

"The Model R's equipped with a power take-off—that's an extreme weak spot in those tractors. If you've got PTO problems in a Model R, you're going to get up front and personal with every part in that transmission. You better have some mechanical abilities within yourself, otherwise you're going to have a ton of time in repairing a PTO. I think that's the first shaft they put in when they built that transmission. It's an angle drive and the engineers just didn't realize how much torque those tractors would develop. But Model Rs were the only ones that had a weak PTO setup." — Albert Ulrich, Renaissance Tractor, Chehalis, Washington

Model 80

The end of the Model R production marked a major transition point in the two-cylinder era. Engineering, tooling, and technology had come of age in the farm machinery industry. The postwar economy in North America and Europe was booming. Tens of thousands of veterans were putting rubber to the ground and steel to the furrow. Bigger was better; more power with more options was in demand for superior implements on larger fields and bigger farms. In its factories, Deere rolled out what the economy wanted: larger tractors with more horsepower than ever dreamed of before. But more than that, it offered a quick progression of new models from very powerful large diesel tractors to, by comparison, toylike tractors for very productive, intense, and small farms. This was a kind of new war. Man and machine made the earth produce more food than ever before. Just 15 years after World War II, the two-cylinder era came to a close. Progress determined that more cylinders were better, and 1960 marked the final year of production for Deere two-cylinder tractors.

During this hectic 15-year period, the mighty 51-horsepower Model R was replaced by the new 67.6-horsepower Model 80 diesel and two successors. The Model 80 was built from late June 1955 through July 1956. The Model 820 went onto the assembly line in July 1956 for two years of production. The last two-cylinder version, the Model 830, was built between August 1958 and July 1960. These were the largest, most powerful two-cylinder diesel tractors Deere produced.

Today, the 4-ton Model 80 is emerging as a highly collectable heavyweight tractor. The Model 80 diesel production run was among the shortest of any in John Deere history. With only 3,500 in the entire series, it is the rarest of the large standard tread, Deere-built tractors. The first of the series rolled out of the Waterloo facility on June 27, 1955, just before the midsummer shutdown. The last tractor of the series was completed just 54 weeks later, on June 11, 1956.

The Model 80 set records and had many new features. In later years, it developed an excellent history as a powerful, reliable workhorse with amazing fuel economy. In Nebraska, the test unit proved to be the most powerful built by Deere to that date. It generated a maximum corrected 67.65 belt horsepower, 61.67 horsepower at the drawbar, and 425 ft-lb of torque at 7,268 rpm—about a third more than the Model R had a few years earlier.

The Model 80 had a significantly stronger three-bearing crankshaft with a center support. The small two-cylinder starting

The king of two-cylinder tractors, the Model 830, is captured in Manitoba sunflowers. This 1959 tractor is equipped with an air precleaner for the carburetor and a new oval muffler that Deere introduced for the 30 series. *Elmer Friesen*

engine from the Model R was replaced with a beefier four-cylinder engine known as the V-4.

The new basic tractor had six forward speeds, a fuel gauge, and a speed-hour meter for a base price of $4,205. Buyers could customize it with a wide variety of options including power steering, live power shaft, dual controls and break-away couplings, remote cylinder, creeper gear, wheel weights, and a cigarette lighter. Most ended up being fully loaded. Dealerships also had several options that could be installed, including a tractor cab, muffler extension, and warning lamps.

New Model 80 owners discovered the old Powr-Trol hydraulic system from the Model R had a major upgrade. Model 80 was the first Deere tractor that could be ordered with

a dual hydraulic box, separate hydraulics for each cylinder, and the ability to separately power two hydraulic circuits. In fact, a tractor could be ordered without PTO and have hydraulics, or it could be ordered with PTO and without hydraulics.

The Model 80 has become a pretty hot item at auction sales over the past decade. Ten years ago it sold for around $4,000, roughly the price of a good Model D or Model R today. When the Model 80 comes up at auction today it is selling for more than $10,000, making it the most valued member of the big standard tread, two-cylinder family. There aren't many Model R tractors coming to the auction block, and that may be part of the reason for the value. It looks like a very good investment.

The V4 starting engine is needed equipment in the northern Great Plains and Canadian prairies.
John Dietz

The 830 has a sophisticated air precleaner and an effective oval muffler.
John Dietz

Twin batteries are hidden under the comfortable seat on the 830.
John Dietz

Standard Model 830 dash and control levers. *Bruce Keller*

Model 820

At first glance, the Model 80 and Model 820 could have been taken as twins. The two looked much the same except for yellow hood side panels on the 820. At this point in 1956, Deere dealers offered a long green line of Models 320, 420, 520, 620, and 720, while clearing stock of a preceding model in each tractor family. On top of that, the new Model 720 diesel had a power boost that gave it nearly as much horsepower as the Model 820.

However, halfway through its two-year production run, the Model 820 tractor was upgraded. Collectors identify these as the black dash 820, as opposed to the green dash 820.

Under the hood, engineers gave the black dash 820 a 12 percent horsepower boost without changing the displacement or operating speed of the engine. Instead, they improved the engine's breathing capacity, modified the pistons for more compression, increased the size of the fuel line, and improved the injectors.

These tractors had Custom Powr-Trol, which was now completely independent of the transmission clutch. They also had PTO, enabling an operator to have two rear hydraulic outlets with an emergency disconnect system. Power steering

was optional. Other options were a creeper gear and Float-Ride seat that could be adjusted for the operator's weight.

With Powr-Trol, the Model 820 weighed 8,150 pounds. Production included 3,100 green dash units and approximately 3,900 black dash tractors.

The Model 820 is easier to find at auction than the Model 80, but it is still not common. It will be less expensive. Around $4,000 to $5,000 will purchase a Model 820 in nice condition at most sales today. It may be a little more at a collectors' sale. One item of note: a fully restored experimental 820 sold at auction in 2004 for $24,000. It was one of only seven experimental units. A year earlier, a fully restored ordinary Model 820 sold for $8,000.

Model 830

Without doubt, the kingpin of the entire John Deere two-cylinder tractor line was the Model 830. It was sometimes known as Mr. Mighty or Big Daddy. Approximately 6,900 were manufactured between 1958 and 1960. However, these were the green-and-yellow farm equivalent to the big late 1950s Cadillac—big, quiet, and comfortable. In fact, the entire 30 series, including the 830, had a new oval muffler that made quieter tractors.

A Model 830 hitch, PTO, and hydraulic ports. Note the operator's step assist. *Bruce Keller*

The Model 830 had the same sheer power as the Model 820 and weighed the same, but it had upgrades for comfort, convenience, and productivity. The PTO, rated for 75.6 horsepower, could handle any load a farm would need. Operators had a more comfortable seat, better controls, and improved instrumentation. There was a foot-pedal accelerator in addition to the usual hand-operated lever accelerator. Many chose to install the new battery-operated, 24-volt electric starter as an option to the V-4 pony engine. The V-4 was a better cold-weather starter. It would warm the diesel engine with shared coolant so the large engine could start more easily in cold weather.

The 830 in good condition is a serious working tractor today if the operator wants it to be. There aren't a lot out there, and the value has been increasing at a nice rate. The average price seems to have risen more than 60 percent in the past decade. The normal price range in 2005 for one of these big tractors at auction was about $8,000 to $9,000. The highest price paid was more than $12,000 for one that was fully loaded at the sale of a private collection in Minnesota.

Models D, R, 80, 820, and 830 Anecdotes

"What's driving the big two-cylinder market in this area is the fact that we have antique tractor pulls at all of our county fairs. Antique tractor pulling is very popular. That's really increasing the value in the R through the 830. The Ds and early diesels are being brought into our area, for the most part, for pulling. We have more and more showing up here that obviously came from the Midwest.

"The 820s and 830s are really popular. I've been at a couple fairs that have two and three 820s and 830s at the same pull. They certainly didn't come from this area. The majority of the tractor pulls in our area are stock pulls. We don't have modified or super-modified.

"That's escalated the value of the bigger tractors because, quite frankly, most people can't pull the things around. We see it here in today's four-wheel-drive market. Most of them didn't have three-point hitches, so they're not being used around the hobby farm. They were just a field-type pulling tractor.

"It's done in different weight classes. The 820s and 830s were the big boys of the John Deere two-cylinder. When you get into that 10,000-plus weight class, there's not many tractors in that class.

"You can put on as many weights as you want. That determines which class you wind up in. They keep the engine stock and the tires stock; they don't want oversize tires.

"There's two types of pulls. They pull on a stone boat, which is basically putting 500- and 1,000-pound concrete blocks on a sled and pulling it. The other is a transfer sled, like you see on TV. We have transfer sled pulls, as well. We have classes for 10,000, 11,000, and 12,000 pounds. That tractor can pull a lot more than its own weight. It wouldn't be uncommon to pull 15,000 or 16,000 pounds with a 10,000-pound tractor. It's amazing to see.

"Results? I think the values of the 820s and 830s have increased just because of the value of what they can pull. If it wasn't for this outlet, I don't believe those tractors would have the draw [in the market] that they do now. In our area [in 2005], an average 830 is going to be in the range of $5,000 to $6,500."

—Terry Robison, R. N. Johnson, Inc., Walpole, New Hampshire

Collectors' Notes

"Probably the biggest thing to watch for is mechanical condition. You can spend a lot of money on a diesel. The only one that had electric start would be the 830; everything else had a cranking engine. If they've got a cranking engine that doesn't run or doesn't run right, you can put a lot of money very easily into a little cranking engine. You can probably spend about as much on that as you can on the big engine." — Gary Uken, Uken Tractor Restoration, Titonka, Iowa

"This stuff is getting harder to come by. Stuff I could get a year ago I can't get today; it doesn't exist. Deere runs out and they quit making it. The biggest thing people want to watch for, when they're buying parts, is when they sub a part over. If they're buying from Deere and they sub a part over, it isn't always exactly the same. For example, on the letter series tractors, just about all of them had white-faced gauges. If you go buy a new gauge from Deere, you're going to get a black-faced gauge. There's a little plug in the hood for where you check the power steering at on the 20 and 30 series tractors. When you get one from Deere, you're going to get a plastic plug instead of a metal plug. The radiator caps even are different than what they did originally, on the Number series through the 30 series. It's just a little radiator cap, like on a car, but it's got a little cover that's spot-welded on. I take the old cover off if it's got the original cap and pop rivet it back onto the new cap." — Gary Uken, Uken Tractor Restoration, Titonka, Iowa

"All the Ds had water valves and antifreeze wasn't used; they used raw water. Boy, watch for freeze cracks big time. A good portion of them went to the boneyard just because they got froze up. Another thing on the early ones with 6.5-inch bore and a horizontal air cleaner, a lot of those weren't in good shape and the cylinder bore really got wore bad. They got a lot of dust in them. They'd run forever because they had huge rings. If they wore the ring lines out on the top, the second or third one would pick up the slack. That's just what happened." – Albert Ulrich, Renaissance Tractor, Chehalis, Washington

"Make sure the tractor starts on both cylinders. They'll sometimes try to start on one cylinder and try to fire on the second cylinder. The Model R main engine didn't fire quite as snappy as the 80, 820, or 830. Make sure that it runs, and runs smooth, doesn't want to hit and miss on one cylinder. Any sign of white smoke means there's unburned fuel or low compression. A lot of times guys will buy a tractor, run it for a while, then all of a sudden start getting some oil spots on the paint job. [It can] look like unburned fuel [but] he's going to end up doing at least some rings. The oil control rings are just absolutely wore out, or sometimes you have a piston with a cracked skirt in it. So check inside the exhaust stack, rub your finger in there, and see if there's any oily residue. It should be just a carbon black surface, and quite dry. There should be a kind of powdered carbon black residue from the exhaust. If it's got any kind of oily film, you want to start checking for any kind of oil seepage that might be around the exhaust manifold bolts or the top of the head. — Albert Ulrich, Renaissance Tractor, Chehalis, Washington

"Diesels have a tendency to have loose flywheels. There's a guy who sells a taper and will put them on for you. I've got a 70 with that taper already in it. They say it fixes it so it will never happen again. All the big diesels had problems if you weren't careful with the flywheel. There's a flywheel cover on that

Model 830. *John Dietz*

side, and if you remove it you can see a little bit if it's really working bad or if you've got a lot of oil coming out of there." — Larry Ott, Fergus Falls, Minnesota

"On the 80, most of the demand is for sheet metal—the fenders, grille, and stuff. You get some calls on engine stuff, but no more than usual. Same with the 820 and 830; calls are mostly about sheet metal and cosmetics. Supplies of sheet metal are getting tough to find. Fenders are real tough to find. Those and grille cowlings, you've got to work with what you've got on them, usually." — Junior Roberts, Steiner Tractor Parts, Flint, Michigan

"If you do run into a flywheel problem in those tractors [the R, 820, or 830], you really want to beware. It's a human-caused problem. Somebody didn't set the flywheel tight enough or whatever when they had it apart. Then you really need to step back and look at it." — Albert Ulrich, Renaissance Tractor, Chehalis, Washington

Specifications

Production & Ratings

Model	Variant	Fuel	Model Years	Number Built	Stars
D	First year	Kerosene	1923	50	*****
D	Spoker	Kerosene	1924	764	****
D	Nickel Hole	Kerosene	1926	2,400	****
D	Corn Borer	Kerosene	1927	440	****
D	Depression	Kerosene	1932	319	****
D	Depression	Kerosene	1933	485	****

Availability
"D" Collectors' Editions—****

4-Star	Number produced	Variant
1924	764	Spoker D
1926	2,400	Nickel Hole D
1927	440	Corn Borer D
1932	319	Depression D
1933	485	Depression D
1935	985	D 3-speed, 12-spline rear axle
1943	557	War Years D
1953	266	Last year

5-Star	Number produced—*****	
1923	50	First year
1928	100	Exhibit A
1930	50	Exhibit B
1953	93	Streeter D

Specifications

Model	D (1924)	R	80	820	830
Base price (1st year)	$1,000	$3,650	$4,200	$4,900	$5,000
Wheelbase (in)	—	—			
Width (in)	56	—	79.5	81	
Height to radiator (in)	56	—	81	80	81
Length (in)	109	147	143	143	143
Weight (in)	4,090	7,400	7,850	7,850	7,850
Front tires/wheels (in)	28x5	7.5x18	7.5x18	7.5x18	7.5x18
Rear tires/wheels (in)	46x12	14x34	15x34	15x34	15x34
Fuel capacity (gal)	18	32.5	32.5	32.5	32.5
Coolant capacity (qt)	13	13.5	8.75	8.0	8.0
Gears forward/reverse	3/1	5/1	6/1	6/1	6/1

Engine/Power Data

Displacement (ci)	465	415	471	471	471
Bore and stroke (in)	6.50x7	5.75x8	6.125x8	6.125x8	6.125x8
Rated rpm	800	1,000	1,125	1,125	1,125
Drawbar horsepower	15	35	46	70	70
Belt/PTO horsepower	27	43	68	76	76
Maximum pull (lb)	3 (14")	6,644	7,394	8,667	8,667
Nebraska Test year	1924	1949	1955	1957	—
Nebraska Test No.	102	406	567	632	—

Parts Replacement/Availability
Parts Prices – Models D, R, 80, 820, 830

	D Low	D High	R Low	R High	80 Low	80 High	820 Low	820 High	830 Low	830 High
Air cleaner intake stack			$60	$98	$60	$98	$60	$98	$60	$98
Amp gauge	$25	$70	$25	$28	$20	$28	$20	$28	$20	$28
Battery box/cover (set)	$95		$105	$135	$105	$129	$105	$140	$100	$140
Camshaft	$194		$120				$155		$155	
Carburetor (rebuilt)	$260	$950								
Carburetor float	$23	$25								
Carburetor kit	$20	$28								
Clutch pulley cover	$26									
Clutch slider disc	$56									
Connecting rod	$30	$175					$98	$111	$98	
Crankshaft							$517		$517	
Cylinder head	$550						$461			
Distributor					$285		$285		$285	
Drag links							$72		$72	
Exhaust pipe	$175	$252	$82	$136	$82	$136	$82	$136	$82	$136
Fender							$101	$142	$142	
Flywheel cover	$95	$105								
Fuel tank							$300			
Generator	$70	$140			$125	$179	$125	$179	$125	$179
Grille screen	$78		$62	$79	$42	$82	$42	$82	$42	$82
Headlight assembly	$37	$75	$37	$67	$57		$57		$57	
Magneto	$249	$365								
Manifold (intake & exhaust)	$295	$300					$61	$97	$61	$97
Muffler			$32	$81	$32	$81	$32	$81	$32	$81
Overhaul kit (pistons, rings, etc.)	$825				$725	$806	$475	$806	$475	$806
Piston							$60		$58	$60
Piston rings					$199		$199	$289	$199	$289

	D Low	D High	R Low	R High	80 Low	80 High	820 Low	820 High	830 Low	830 High
Radiator					$401		$188	$401	$188	$401
Radiator cap	$19	$90	$19	$25	$13	$15	$15		$15	
Radiator core	$252	$302	$252		$129	$350	$129	$350	$129	$350
Seat cushion (bottom)	$28	$50	$28	$60	$28	$60	$28	$60	$28	$60
Sediment bowl	$45	$55			$18	$24	$18	$24	$18	$24
Spark plug wire (set)	$11	$17	$11	$17	$13		$13		$13	
Starter	$200	$299	$170	$229	$125	$150	$220	$449	$220	$449
Steering wheel	$44	$75	$44	$75	$49	$140	$49	$140	$49	$140
Toolbox	$30	$50			$71	$72	$71	$72	$71	$72
Voltage regulator	$36	$52	$37				$42		$42	
Water pump					$83	$146	$83	$146	$83	$146

Special Traits

Series	D					R	80	820	830
Model	Early	Mid	Late	Styled	Streeter				
Total Built (197,857)	23,135	55,929	33,034	46,916	92	21,293	3,485	7,080	6,893
Collectability	**	*	*	*	*****	*	**	*	**
Reports	81					29	12	31	25
Avg. sales value 2004–2005	$4,324				$3,783	$9,908	$5,150	$7,739	
2005 High	$17,000					$5,250	$13,750	$11,500	$12,250
Record High	$17,000					$6,250	$13,750	$11,500	$12,250

SPECIFICATIONS

	Early	Mid	Late	Styled	Streeter	R	80	820	830
Base price (1st year)	$1,112	$1,075	$1,125	$2,422		$3,764	$4,205	$4,900	$5,000
Weight (lb):	4,000	4,164	5,114	5,269	5,269	7,400	7,850	7,850	7,850
Width (in)	56					79.5	86.6	79.5	79.5
Height to radiator (in)	56					78	79.5	81	81
Length (in)	109					147	137	143	143
Front tires (in)	28x5					7.50x18	7.50x18	7.50x18	7.50x18
Rear tires (in)	46x12					15-34	15-34	15-34	15-34
Fuel capacity (gal)	18					22	32.5	32.5	32.5
Cooling capacity (qt)						13.5	8.75	8.75	8.75
Gears forward/reverse	2-1	3-1	3-1	3-1	3-1	5-1	6-1	6-1	6-1

ENGINE / POWER DATA

	Early	Late	R	80	820
Nebraska Test No.	102	236	406	567	632
Nebraska Test Year	4/11/2024	6/26/1935	4/19/1949	10/27/1955	10/14/1957
Rated rpm	800	900	1,000	1,125	1,125
Bore and stroke (in)	6.5x7	6.75x7	5.75x8	6.12x8	6.12x8
Displacement (ci)					
Belt/PTO horsepower	30.4	41.59	51	67.6	75.6
Drawbar horsepower	22.53	30.74	45.7	61.8	69.66
Maximum pull	3,277	4,037	6,644	7,394	8,667
Shipping weight (lb)		5,690	10,398	11,485	11,995

Average Sale Values 1995 to 2010 (Actual and Projected)

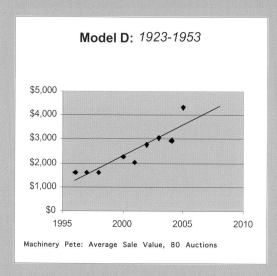

Model D: *1923-1953*

Machinery Pete: Average Sale Value, 80 Auctions

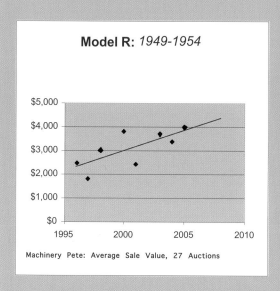

Model R: *1949-1954*

Machinery Pete: Average Sale Value, 27 Auctions

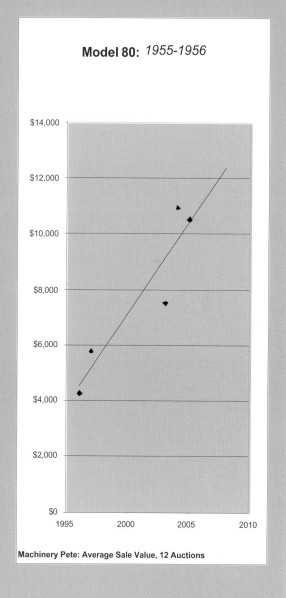

Model 80: *1955-1956*

Machinery Pete: Average Sale Value, 12 Auctions

Average Sale Values 1995 to 2010 (Actual and Projected)

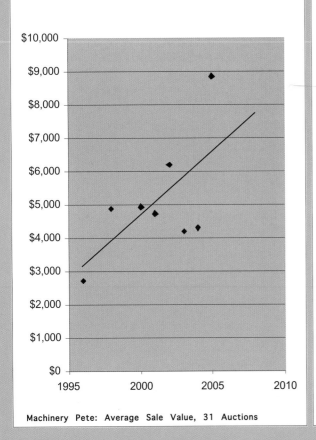

Model 820: *1956-1958*

Machinery Pete: Average Sale Value, 31 Auctions

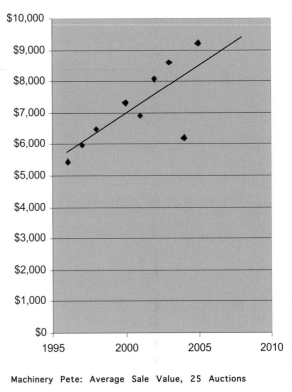

Model 830: *1958-1960*

Machinery Pete: Average Sale Value, 25 Auctions

1937 Golden D

This Golden 1937 D is the very same tractor that John Deere built in 1937 to help commemorate its centennial celebration. It was restored by its owner, Charles English, of Evansville, Indiana. English found no mention of the Golden D in John Deere archives and the only mention of it was in an article in *Implement & Tractor* magazine. With clues from the article, English began looking for the special tractor.

Josiah Gooden and Son Hardware in Kingfisher, Oklahoma, was a John Deere dealer in 1937. The owner saw the Golden D in Kansas City at the John Deere Branch House and bid on it. Since the dealership had an outstanding tractor sales record that year, Gooden and Son was allowed to purchase the Golden D. The owner figured it would have good merchandising and advertising value. The tractor arrived in time for the Gooden dealership's 25th anniversary and attracted much attention. The tractor was sold after the promotion was over. There was a race to purchase the Golden D, which resulted in a close heat between a Mr. Hancock and J. J. Haffner, a Kingfisher farmer. Hancock finally won out and purchased the special tractor. Haffner purchased a standard Green D and took his defeat in good grace.

Grandson George Gooden assisted English in finding the Golden D, and after seven years of negotiation, he bought it from the Beacher family in Kingfisher, Oklahoma. The tractor was in pieces and in need of a full restoration. During its useful life it was painted John Deere green, but the gold-leaf paint was still under the green paint. After 400 hours of shop time, the tractor was fully restored and is in perfect shape.

(See www.okjdclub.com/featgold.mydop)

A 1951 Model A row-crop in Missouri. *Ron Jungmeyer*

Chapter 3

Models A, 60, 620, 630

Deere's design engineers soon were at work on a row-crop concept once the company was successfully selling the standard tread Model D. Between 1928 and 1937, three fundamental sizes of row-crop tractors were developed for production at Waterloo. The tread of the row-crop tractor could be standard, but most were not. The row-crop tractors in this chapter are the midsize family. They were introduced in 1934, during the middle of the row-crop development era. Some of these tractors were so successful and popular that many survive today. They are among the least costly investments for a home-restoration project and ideal for the backyard hobbyist who's ready to get grease on his fingers. On the other hand, some are exceptionally rare. A very rare 1959 Model 630 came up at auction in 2005. It sold for a record-setting $141,000. A restorable 1940s Model A in fair condition still can be purchased at auction for well under $1,000.

For perspective, while the Model D series was in its heyday, both farmers and engineers recognized a need for other types of tractors. The Model D had tremendous power for plowing from sunrise to sunset in broad open fields, but it was limited compared to the diverse needs of farming in North America. Many farmers wanted a general-purpose tractor for a range of applications on a single farm. Some wanted smaller tractors for smaller farms. Others wanted tractors for row-crops and for orchards. Deere and other tractor manufacturers responded and started to introduce new models about five years after the Model D came into production. Deere's first entry, a General Purpose tractor, was introduced in 1928, about a year before the stock market crashed. As the economy recovered in the late 1930s, Deere introduced a third family of even larger row-crop tractors in 1937. One more family was to be introduced at Waterloo, so from 1937

to 1947, the Waterloo factory was building five separate streams of tractors on its assembly lines.

The Model A was introduced in 1934. The A and its successors, Models 60, 620, and 630, were manufactured through 1960. They were large and powerful, though less bulky than the big kerosene-fueled Model D or later diesel-fueled Model R family.

These midsize row-crop tractors were incredibly popular. Deere built 425,000 of them, averaging about 18,000 annually over the 24-year production cycle. They were coming off the Waterloo assembly lines at rates of about 100 a day and were being distributed to nearly every corner of North America as well as into Europe. Eventually, they accounted for nearly a third of all Deere two-cylinder tractors. These row-crop tractors were built in many variations for an array of applications. Although this chapter heading identifies only four models, there were at least 61 versions in the family. They are classed by model, style, fuel, and application (e.g., row-crop, orchard, standard, etc.). Serious collectors can develop a personal library of information on the tractors in this single chapter, as well as those featured in Chapters 4, 5, and 6.

Most row-crop tractors burned gasoline or a combination of gasoline and distillate. For collectors, fuel can be an important distinguishing characteristic. The terms "gasoline" and "diesel" seem to speak for themselves, but younger collectors need a quick introduction to some older terms such as tractor fuel, distillate, and all-fuel.

Kerosene, the standard fuel for Model D tractors, was mostly derived from coal. Distillate, or tractor fuel, came a long a bit later. It was similar to kerosene, but was derived from petroleum and had a lower octane than gasoline. The engine needed to be really hot in order to vaporize and burn

Rare French and Hecht spoke wheels, front and rear, plus rubber tires, adorn this prized, perfectly restored 1937 Model A. This model is famous for its narrow radiator and fuel tank. It was introduced as the General Purpose tractor and evolved into nine subgroups and through 19 styling changes over its 19-year history. The first of three styled versions was introduced in 1938. *Ron Jungmeyer*

distillate. You couldn't start a tractor with it. Designers built a workable and more economical fuel system by putting two fuel tanks on these tractors. Generally, these became known as all-fuel tractors. Operators started the engine with gasoline from a small tank and once it was warmed up they switched a valve to the distillate tank. The tractor didn't develop as much power, distillate was much cheaper than gasoline at the time. After the two-cylinder era, when gasoline became as cheap as tractor fuel, the all-fuel engines were discontinued and engine compression was increased to get the full horsepower potential from gasoline.

A few of the row-crop tractors ran on liquid propane (LP) gas. LP gas burned hotter, generated more power, and was available at an economical price in some southern U.S. farming areas. Deere records indicate 11,000 LP gas, midsize row-crop tractors were built, or about 2.5 percent of the total production. Generally, these are harder to find and more valuable than models with conventional fuel.

In the 1930s, options and accessories became common for row-crop tractors emerging from Waterloo. A rule of thumb for today's collector: it is always cheaper to buy a tractor with the options on it than it is to add them later. If you want options when you buy a two-cylinder tractor, start with as many as you can get.

This is one of 220 tractors in a styled A variation. These were the last of the unsold, unstyled 1938 Model A tractors. They were sent back through the assembly line and offered as a 1939 styled A tractor. This one was photographed in Missouri. *Eddie Campbell*

Iowa restoration expert Gary Uken warned, "If you're buying a row-crop tractor and you want a rockshaft, a three-point, a wide front axle, weights, and fenders, you're better off looking for a tractor with that equipment on it versus buying a plain stripped tractor and then adding it all. Options add up real quick. It's easily $1,000 a pop for a wide front end or fenders and lights. The three-point hitch is probably going to be $1,000 to $1,500. Front weights will be about $1,000. If you do the hydraulic box, there's another $800 to $1,000. If you add all that, it's a lot of dollars."

Model A

John Deere's first row-crop tractor, the Model A, was a huge success for Waterloo. For collectors, it's a good introductory tractor but not likely to return cash on the invested hours of love and learning. Individual units, like the first or last, have high value by virtue of being nearly one of a kind. As a series, the Model A itself is one of the least valued among surviving John Deere two-cylinder tractors simply because so many survive. Deere manufactured more than 65,000 of the unstyled early A tractors between 1934 and 1939. It followed this with nearly 100,000 early styled A tractors through 1947 and an additional 90,000 late styled A tractors to the end of the series in 1953.

The original Model A was a General Purpose tractor with a two-wheel tricycle front axle. In the two-plow class it was the first tractor with an adjustable tread width for its rear wheels. Rear wheel spacing could be 56 to 80 inches wide, giving farmers flexibility to work in 40- or 42-inch rows of corn or cotton. It also offered hydraulic Power Lift, an extremely important option for implements. Power Lift could raise and gently lower an implement at row-end, eliminating a back-breaking task for growers and increasing the ability to do about 10 percent more land per day.

Deere tested 10 preproduction prototypes of the unstyled A in spring 1933, designating them as AA tractors. The AA tractors were rebuilt into regular production tractors and issued new serial numbers. With very positive and clear results, Deere's directors approved full production of the three-speed Model A in late July 1933 at a rate of 50 tractors per day and set aside the four-speed transmission that had been considered.

The 1934 Model A was really an upgrade from the General Purpose Wide Tread (GPWT) that Deere started building before the Depression. On the assembly line Deere allowed 1,100 of the first Model A units to slip through with a mixed designation. The few that survive in collections are known as the GP-A tractor. The decal on the hood said "GP" and the serial number tag bore the words "General Purpose," followed by the new Model A serial number. Collectors lucky enough to find an unstyled 1934 A with the GP tag should insure that tractor for at least an extra $1,000. One dealer commented, "It's unbelievable how much guys will give for the GP tag." One Model A that he described as a "basket case with a GP tag"

This beautiful 1952 Model A in Minnesota has all the bells and whistles of its era, including Powr-Trol and Roll-O-Matic front end. It had adjustable rear wheels with individual brakes; six-speed transmission plus reverse; a spring-mounted, weight-adjustable operator's seat; and other creature comforts. *Peter Easterlund*

was purchased for $6,000 and hauled more than 1,000 miles to the collector's home. "Without the tag that tractor would have been a 1934 open fan shaft A, so it probably would have sold for $3,500 to $4,000. The tag made the difference."

According to the Machinery Pete database (www. machinerypete.com), the highest auction value for a plain Model A prior to 2006 was $20,000 at a June 2003 auction. It was described as, "The 59th JD A produced, original HC 125, early rockshaft, center fill tank, early seat bracket, all of the correct hard-to-find parts, restored, SN #410059."

The open fan shaft, mentioned above, was a weak point on the Model A of 1934–1935. It was prone to breaking because there was nothing to support the front of the fan shaft. When it got out of balance or if the clutch wore, the housing would end up broken and replaced with an enclosed fan shaft. In mid-1935 Deere began building an enclosed fan

shaft and fixed the problem. Few of the early models with open fan shafts survive today. They are easily recognized and a prize for a collector. An unstyled A from that era with the original complete open fan shaft in good shape is worth, on the market, probably a third more than the value of one that's been replaced with an enclosed fan shaft. If any of these components are missing or broken, the collector will be hard-pressed to achieve a complete restoration with original parts, although reproduction components may be available.

Wheels are a third variable in the unstyled A series. The unstyled Model A can have spoke wheels, steel wheels, or cast-iron wheels in several combinations. Wheels with round spokes are the hardest to find and bring the most money. A pair of restorable round spoke wheels for a Model A (or a Model B) can sell for around $2,000, whether a tractor is attached or not. The front wheels will bring $800 to $1,000.

A wheel with a cast rim is worth considerably less. The least valued is a cut-down steel wheel. These were trimmed with a torch and grinder to hold a conventional rim and rubber tire. It will be costly and perhaps not worth the investment to restore a tractor in that condition to factory condition. Flat-spoke wheels were an over-the-counter option to replace the original steel wheels with rubber tires.

Axle splines are a fourth variable in the unstyled A series. On the early A, axles had 10 splines. In mid or late 1937, Deere started putting 12 slightly narrower splines on the same axles for early A tractors. Around 1942 Deere changed the design again to have 15 splines and kept that pattern until the end of production. Know your spline size if you're shopping for a wheel or axle from that era. Some collectors may want to have one tractor with each spline style.

Product development for the styled A slowed during the war years, although there still were differences from year to year. The 1941 A did have a new six-speed transmission for the models with rubber tires. Steel-wheel versions were restricted to four gears because for these tractors high speeds were considered dangerous. The 1941 Model A also had a new magneto (the Wico C) and a new carburetor (the DLTX 53). The changes were successful and Deere built more than 12,000 of these tractors in 1941.

A Model A Hi-Crop at an exhibition day run by the Rough and Tumble Association in Pennsylvania. *Jacob Merriwether*

This is one of 26 ANH tractors built by Waterloo, starting in late December 1937. The AN had a single nose wheel and the ANH was the high-clearance version. They were built for California vegetable growers. *Bruce Keller*

Late in 1945, after the war was over, Deere offered its first major product development for all three families of row-crop tractors in about five years. This was the new Powr-Trol hydraulic system. For the first time, this gave farmers a system that could power a hydraulic cylinder while providing precise positioning. Powr-Trol initially controlled the rockshaft on the row-crop tractor. Supply was limited for a couple years, but many tractors were retrofitted.

In 1947, the late styled A offered Powr-Trol as a $149 option. Demand was overwhelming. After that point, hydraulic Power Lift became standard equipment on row-crop tractors. The 1947 Model A also carried the battery under the seat and had a more open operator's station.

With the noted exceptions, the average price at auction for the garden-variety Model A in running condition in 2005 was around $1,500. Restoring one of these was a labor of love rather than an investment. The upward margin for one in premium condition and with cast wheels was probably no more than $2,500 at auction, which is enough profit to cover a few parts without anything for the labor of restoration. On the other hand, values in private sales may be much different. One restoration expert said, "The 1935s through 1938s are getting really hard to find, and the value is up somewhat. Your normal restored row-crop A in good shape, at the high end, probably is going to be around $4,500 to $5,000."

Still, the motivations of collectors are as diverse and personal as imagination. One of the big motivators is the sound of the old two-cylinder tractor. Comparing a Model A to a similar, slightly smaller Model B, one collector said, "I specialize in the unstyled stuff. The A and B look identical; the A is just a bigger tractor. They look the same and they made a lot of both, but a lot of people like the sound of the A—it's got a real good throaty bark to it. That's my personal favorite, out of all the tractors that I have."

Model A Variations

Model A variations are a different matter for collectors. Many of the 25 subgroups from the garden-variety Model A are highly collectable due to low production numbers and general disappearance over the intervening decades.

Model designation needs a quick introduction at this point. The ordinary row-crop A had two front wheels riding on a single post attached to the chassis casting.

A row-crop Model A could have only one front wheel and it looked like a big tricycle; it was called the AN, for narrow.

An adjustable-width front axle was needed. This could be wider than the rear wheel spacing and was designated as AW.

Some were given extra height for working in taller row-crops, as well as the single nose wheel. These high-clearance tractors were designated ANH.

Carl Morgan bought this Model AO tractor on July 18, 1951, for his Arkansas peach orchard. It's still in the family and has been lovingly restored. *David Morgan*

This 1938 Model AOS all-fuel with electric start is a fully streamlined version of the AR and is ready for orchard work. The exhaust is under the tractor. Separate rear wheel brakes improve maneuverability. *Bruce Keller*

A standard tread, non-row-crop version of the Model A, the AR (R for regular tread) was introduced in 1937. It was lower and heavier without the hydraulic lift and was fitted with a single brake. This is a 1951 AR version on steel at a rural tractor museum in Manitoba. *John Dietz*

Some needed both height and adjustable-width front axles. These models became the AWH.

If the A had a solid beam axle under the front pedestal with fixed wheel spacing or standard tread, it could be a good option to the larger Model D. It was designated an AR.

A similar but small set of tractors with standard tread was developed for work in orchards. These were streamlined to prevent snagging on branches and were known as the AO or AOS tractors.

A truly rare member of the family at auction will draw bids from virtually anywhere in the world. The rarest are the early ANH and early AWH versions. Only 26 and 27, respectively, were built during one short season in 1938 just before

styled models were introduced. The value of the early ANH or AWH models is hard to estimate. However, a pristine, fully restored, gas-engine late styled Model A Hi-Crop set the sales record at auction in 2003 for the entire Model A family. It sold for $40,000 and was one of 246 manufactured.

In the unstyled A series, variations were introduced between 1935 and 1938 as the AN, ANH, AO, AOS, AR, AW, and AWH. The AN was a true tricycle tractor with only a single front wheel. Few were made, and survivors are very collectable. The AW, a wide front axle version, was added to the line in 1935, at the same time as the AN. Two years later, Deere offered high-crop, rubber-tired versions called the ANH or AWH. Only 53 were produced, and each survivor is truly cherished. The AWH with its widely spaced front wheels and high-crop clearance stands out in nearly any crowd.

Other introductions in 1935 were the standard AR[3] and the AO, or orchard version of the A. The AO was streamlined in 1937 to prevent damage to trees and became the AOS. Both the AR and AO make excellent collector tractors, although the AO is much harder to find and is relatively more valuable.

The AR, with its fixed, matching wheel spacing, was a popular alternative to the bigger, diesel-fuel R family. It was designed for field work and is a good family tractor today. For an inexperienced or young operator, it made a very fine, user-friendly training tractor. The operator was closer to the ground. It had completely enclosed fenders and a nice, safe operator's platform, including an innovative footbrake on the platform. It was easy to get on, easy to operate, and easy to get off. It's also a bargain today with a maximum auction value of around $5,000.

The AO was a twin to the AR, with modifications for orchards, but few were produced. It had twin turning brakes rather than a single brake pedal. It had louvers on the hood so that branches would slide up and over. The AR's vertical exhaust stack and air breather pipes were removed for clearance under low-hanging branches. Few AO and AOS models go into auction; high prices at auction recorded were $10,000 for the AO in 2005 and $16,000 for the AOS in 2001.

Variations on the early styled A line included AN, ANH, AW, and AWH. The late styled A series included AN, AW, AO, AR, and AH designations. The A Hi-Crop was advertised as the "Famous Model A on Stilts" with 33 inches of vertical clearance at the axles. It became the best-selling high-crop tractor. Deere sold just over 425 of these.

Serial number research is the best way to accurately identify the original configuration for many tractors. Published lists of serial numbers enable collectors and tractor buyers to identify tractor models and years. Detailed information on original configuration for the specific tractor normally is available on request from the Two-Cylinder® Club.

The styled A and styled AW are sometimes not what they seem, says Texas restoration specialist Kenny Earman:

"If you get an early A with a wide front end, like a 1939 to 1946, you can pretty much bet that it was originally an AW because the casting is cast into the front. Those AWs with the anteater nose are a little more valuable than the A that just happens to have a wide front end.

Another AR, a 1952 model on rubber, resides in a private family collection in Missouri. Same assembly line, different world.
Eddie Campbell

Right: A 1936 Model AR standard gas. *John Dietz*

Below left: Grille screens and radiators are available for the unstyled AR tractors at reasonable prices. *John Dietz*

Below: Open the brass petcock valve beside the spark plug to release compression before turning the flywheel. *John Dietz*

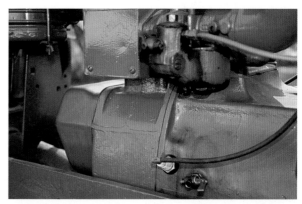

With a logo like this on the radiator housing, there's no hiding who built it. *John Dietz*

A wide-front version of Model A, the AW, was introduced in 1935. This one was delivered to Deere inventory on April 27, 1944, according to a certificate issued by the Two-Cylinder Club to the New York owner. *Keith Morey*

"If you see a convertible pedestal, you don't know whether the tractor was originally a tricycle front. Somebody may have bought this wide front and put it on. If it's not a true AW, it's not as collectable. Without actually doing serial number research and getting the archive information, you don't know whether the particular late AW truly came equipped that way from the factory.

"And it's the same with the single front wheel. That pedestal was easily changed. Just because a late styled A has a wide front end, don't think you've got a rare tractor without checking the archive information."

Model A Buyers' Guide

"Number one: is it running or not? If you buy a tractor that isn't running, you're taking a big chance because you don't know what's wrong. The transmission could be bad, or the rear end. There's no way of knowing just by looking from the outside."

"Your sheet metal and things like that are readily available for your early unstyled tractors. If you have to go into the gears [for replacements], it's getting very expensive. Your internal engine parts, too, like your heads, your blocks, your crankshafts are quite expensive for the same reason—they don't make them anymore."

"A lot of times you run into worn clutch linkage [in the unstyled A]. When I get a tractor, usually the linkage is worn quite a lot. Also, most of the time it won't have very good brakes. In the styled A, there's nothing that stands out [for repairs]. They're a good tractor, really are. I don't think any had serious weaknesses."

— Kenny Earman, Early Iron Restoration, Mt. Pleasant, Texas

"Unless it's super rare or unless it's grandpa's old tractor, buy the best tractor you can find. Your initial dollar is the cheapest money you spend. There's exceptions. If you get a hi-crop A with a bad engine and transmission, you can find those parts. As long as the rare parts are still with it, you can build it up again from another tractor that isn't rare. On a common tractor it's not cost-effective to do that; you can't afford to hire it done."

— Ron Jungmeyer, Jungmeyer Tractor Restoration Service, Russellville, Missouri

"You need to have a low production tractor to get your money out. It's very hard to get your money out of any kind of common row-crop tractor. If you do [the work] yourself, it's going to be a push, probably, and you might break even. If you do a proper, ground-up restoration where you tear it apart, inspect everything, and rebuild everything, you'll probably never get your money out except on the super-rare ones. The best thing to do as an investment is to save your money and buy something rare. Some people just want something to play with. From what I've found, you are better off buying a restored tractor versus buying one that needs paint, tires, and an overhaul. By the time you get done doing that, even doing it yourself, you're going to have a lot of money in the tractor."

— Gary Uken, Uken Tractor Restoration, Titonka, Iowa

"A late styled A would be the best in this chapter for a new collector. You're looking at about $1,500 for one, as opposed to $3,500 to $6,000 for a Model 630 in the same condition, and parts are pretty readily available. An A isn't that popular, but if you want one to have a good time with, they'll do most anything the newer ones will do—go as fast, run as good, look almost as nice."

— Don Doeden, Cook, Nebraska

A Model AWH is in storage at the Keller Museum. Like the ANH, only 27 were built over a six-month period. They served the needs of California vegetable growers. *Bruce Keller*

A pristine 1955 Model 60 row-crop tractor with Powr-Trol, Roll-O-Matic, and power steering. The 60 had a live PTO, live hydraulics, an early three-point hitch, a simplified rear wheel adjustment, 12-volt electric system, and optional long axles with dished wheels for 104-inch spacing. *Peter Easterlund*

"The easy way to spot an AO is the fact that all of them had turning brakes. You could convert an AR, take off the exhaust stack and the breather pipe, put an AO hood on it. But if it doesn't have twin turning brakes, you can immediately tell it's an AR and not an AO.

"I'd get hold of an unstyled A. Most of them were hand-start. They're just so simple. They don't have a water pump. You don't have to worry about a battery or starter or alternator. The fact that it's a hand-start makes it unusual. At a tractor show or parade, it really draws a crowd when you open those petcocks and throw that flywheel over. And, the As are relatively common. A lot of people are making aftermarket parts for them. It's easy to get used original parts. The only

sheet metal is in the hood. That can be replaced, and there's even less cost for painting. In the long run I think the value of the unstyled A will do better than the styled A, which is more common."

— Terry Robison, R. N. Johnson, Inc., Walpole, New Hampshire

"They didn't make a whole lot of single fronts and wide fronts at the factory, but I think a lot of them got changed over at the dealership or the farmer went to the dealer and ordered the front end. If you want a legitimate one, you've got to check the serial number to see if it left the factory with it."

— Ron Jungmeyer, Jungmeyer Tractor Restoration Service, Russellville, Missouri

Model 60

The Model 60 and Model 50 were introduced officially with much fanfare on June 20, 1952. Key selling points for these three-plow tractors were the dual carburetion, Quick-Change wheel tread, and Roll-O-Matic front end. The Model 60 was the successor to Deere's very popular late styled A, and the first of five Number series tractor models introduced by Deere & Co. between 1952 and 1956. During its five production years, Deere manufactured 61,000 Model 60 tractors. About 80 percent were row-crop tractors with gasoline engines. Today, the Model 60 row-crop is a one-star tractor in respect to its collectability. It usually is reasonably priced and still is readily available in many areas of the eastern United States and in southern Ontario. In fact, some are still in service, hauling balers on farms in New England. They are gaining in popularity at some of the tractor pulls. They have a little more horsepower than some of the styled A models and pull well.

A few of the later Model 60 row-crop tractors have a three-point hitch (commonly called the 800 or 801 hitch). The three-point hitch makes it more utilitarian, as well as more collectable. If the hitch is in good shape, the tractor value should increase at least $500 or more.

Any of the remaining Model 60s that can be found are worth at least two stars or more for a collector. The Model 60 was produced with three engines and in five versions. The all-fuel, row-crop version was most popular, with more than 4,400 manufactured. The row-crop and hi-crop models could be ordered with an LP engine, which was a $245 option chosen for 3,800 units. Other versions were the low-seat standard, high-seat standard, hi-crop, and orchard.

The Model 60 standard version was similar to the AR that it succeeded, while the Model 60 orchard replaced the AO. At midstream, Deere raised the height of the driver's seat on the standard tread and orchard versions of the Model 60. It had produced about 1,900 low-seat standard units prior to December 1954, and only a handful of these were in the orchard version. Deere also produced a few low-seat standard Model 60 tractors with its newest innovation: power steering. Any of these variations are hard to find and worth an extra star for collectors.

The later high-seat standard for 1955 and 1956 had power steering, slightly taller tires, and a seat design similar to the new Model 70 row-crop series. The higher sitting position offered better operator comfort, protection, field of vision,

The Model 60, produced from 1952 to 1956, was a revolutionary change from the Model A series it replaced. It was the first John Deere to give farmers a choice of gasoline, all-fuel (distillate), or LPG-powered engines. This one was restored to pristine condition by Missouri specialist Ron Jungmeyer. *Ron Jungmeyer*

This Model 60 orchard in British Columbia is obviously well cared for. A wraparound, vertical-pleat radiator or grille was introduced in 1949 on the Model 60. The radiator, pressurized with a water pump and thermostatic control, also was new. *Leon Rumpf*

larger tires, and greater vertical clearance. It also offered an optional adjustable-tread front axle, combining the best of the standard and row-crop features. For collectors, the change is a notable difference. Most of the standard all-fuel models were shipped overseas. Only 15 each of the low-seat and high-seat versions stayed in North America.

The Model 60 Hi-Crop is the rarest and most valuable version. Production by fuel type was all-fuel: 135; gasoline: 62; and LP gas: 15. The hi-crop tractors were shipped to Florida, Alabama, and Louisiana.

True to form for Deere, the Waterloo assembly lines turned out many versions of the Model 60 beyond the named variations. Some were integral to the rest of the series, and others were options that farmers and dealers requested for specific units. For instance, configuration choices in row-crop Model 60s in late 1952 included gasoline or all-fuel engines, a new live PTO ($135) or transmission-driven PTO, and solid front-wheel assembly or Roll-O-Matic front-wheel assembly ($55). The all-fuel versions gained the dual-carburetion system in January 1953. In 1954, Deere began offering a revolutionary three-point hitch, known as the 800, that was designed by the Yakima Works and Waterloo engineers as a replacement for the No. 2100 carrier for implements. It proved to be popular and was upgraded in 1956 to the 801 Traction-Trol hitch, which was able to transfer weight to the rear wheels for integral attachments.

As with the Model A, Model 60 buyers could choose a standard one-piece front pedestal or an optional two-piece pedestal. The two-piece option enabled a variety of front ends to be fitted, including a 38-inch fixed-tread front axle. The two-piece option proved most popular and became standard on 1954 row-crop models, while the one-piece pedestal was phased out. Late in 1954, Deere began offering factory-installed power steering ($125) on the Model 60 row-crop and hi-crop tractors. It was a huge change at the time and offered one-finger steering in virtually any field condition.

Sheet metal on the Model 60 is something to examine in detail. At a distance, the Model 60s may look the same, but the series had three versions of the hood and gas tank. The filling cap on the gas tank dictated the style of hood. The earliest hood was like its predecessor, the Model A. The late hood was similar to the 620. There's little demand for the Model 60, and aftermarket suppliers haven't bothered with producing the Model 60 sheet metal. If you want the hood to look pretty and prefer a nose that's clean, put more value on finding sheet metal than on the engine. It's easier and probably less costly to replace the engine than the nose pieces.

Overall, the Model 60 was a good tractor. Mechanically, unless it's using oil or belching smoke, it probably will be as reliable as you want it to be. Its collectability and value probably will increase as time goes by.

Rear details of the 60 orchard. Classic clamshell fenders, wide tires for low impact on orchard rows, and a rear backup light were included on this tractor. *Leon Rumpf*

An over-the-dash view from the Model 60 orchard. This tractor is as clean and pristine as mountain air on a spring morning. *Leon Rumpf*

A 1956 Model 620 row-crop is restored to perfection. The front width can be adjusted with pins through holes on either side of the axle. *John Dietz*

Value of the Model 60 has increased gradually. The 1996 Model 60 that was worth $1,500 may bring $2,500 today. Higher values at auction tend to push $4,000, but many are low-cost, entry-level models under $2,000. The very best have brought from $10,000 to $57,000 at auction in the past five years.

Model 60 Buyers' Guide
"Some 60s were available with a three-point hitch. I remember when I could buy them for $300; now they're up to $1,000. Besides making the tractor more valuable, it's useful now because you can put on a rake or a grader blade and use it around the yard. You might convince your wife that,

This Model 620 all-fuel Hi-Crop is one of only 16 that were made. The other two tractors were exported. *Bruce Keller*

This John Deere two-cylinder tractor that looks like it was crossed with a spaceship is also known as the Model 620 orchard. *Ron Jungmeyer*

if you buy this collector tractor, you can still plow the driveway with it.

"For Model 60, you want to be sure that the clutch engages and disengages well. They have a tendency to either wear or stick inside the clutch housing."
— Terry Robison, R. N. Johnson, Inc., Walpole, New Hampshire

"It's funny; in the Number series, the 60s are the cheapest tractor you can buy right now. If you're buying horsepower, it's cheap, cheap horsepower. One reason is that they don't have a very good hydraulic system. A lot of them don't have the three-point hitch, either. Those two things kind of hurt that model."
— Kenny Earman, Early Iron Restoration, Mt. Pleasant, Texas

"There were several good things about the 60 series. One, you could turn the hydraulic system on or off. You can turn it off at the engine by means of gears. It saves gas and saves wear and tear. Another good thing was power steering. It came out in 1954 or late 1953. Having power steering probably was the biggest advancement that John Deere made in that series."

— Kenny Earman, Early Iron Restoration, Mt. Pleasant, Texas

"I'm not sure why, but in the [Model] 60s and 70s, you can still buy a good-running propane tractor for $1,200 to $1,500. That's not restored, but it's not much money, either."

— Kenny Earman, Early Iron Restoration, Mt. Pleasant, Texas

"A lot of people will just turn their noses up at a 60. I don't know where that has come from. They're basically the same tractor as a 620. That tractor, fixed up, is just as nice looking as anything with a yellow stripe. It just isn't highly sought after. Basically, it's a sleeper. It's never caught on in all the years I've been collecting. I don't think it ever will to the extent of the yellow stripe stuff."

— Ron Jungmeyer, Jungmeyer Tractor Restoration Service, Russellville, Missouri

"In the 1950s, they built a 60 low-seat standard, which doesn't catch a lot of attention for some reason. They only built about 1,900 of them. Then they built a 60 high-seat in a little lower production numbers yet. Those are a nice sharp tractor.

"The 60 series had a serious block-cracking problem. The 60 came out with a block casting number of A 4320 R, and if you're looking at one you want to really, really shake it down. They used the same block as the late styled A, but they had more block problems because they were making more horsepower. That block is easy to identify: it will have two bolts in the middle rather than one. Some replacement blocks Deere produced had the same part number but they had a little more meat up inside the block and it helped. When you find a 60 with a Powerblock, 9 out of 10 times you can figure that the original block cracked. Really pay attention to the integrity of that block if you're buying a Model 60. Look for any sign of moisture in your exhaust and whether that engine on startup wants to miss on one cylinder for a little bit."

— Albert Ulrich, Renaissance Tractor, Chehalis, Washington

Model 620

The Model 620 was unveiled as successor to the Model 60 for 1957. It was manufactured for two years and then replaced in 1959 by the 630. The sheet metal was unchanged from the last edition of the Model 60 but the paint was different. The Model 620 had the new two-tone, green-and-yellow paint scheme associated with the 20 series, but under the hood and paint it was a very different tractor.

The 620 had about 20 percent more horsepower and consumed less fuel than the Model 60. With more pep than the Model 60, the 620 could pull slightly wider equipment or it could pull a bit faster. It had a much better engine block with aluminum pistons. Cylinder bore stayed at 5.5 inches and the 6.375-inch stroke was slightly shorter, but the engine speed was cranked up 15 percent to 1,125 rpm. Engineers had moved the spark plugs to the cylinder head and put in a distributor drive pad that enabled it to be driven by the camshaft rather than governor gearing. They had strengthened the whole tractor to cope with the extra power and had eliminated the old petcocks for hand-start.

Along with the paint and power, drivers found themselves more comfortable. They could order the Model 620 with the new Float-Ride seat that had two foam cushions and a shock absorber. Hydraulics introduced on the Model 80 were incorporated into the Model 620. Custom Powr-Trol was a big improvement and allowed control of three separate hydraulic circuits. These included front and rear rockshafts, two separate remote cylinders, or a new three-point hitch with top-link sensing for load and depth.

The Model 620 was available in configurations familiar to Model 60 owners as row-crop, standard, and hi-crop. Standard tread was a continuation of the high-seat 60 standard. Most options were available for all three versions. The Model 620 Standard did not have the front rockshaft, but that feature was found on the 620 orchard.

The 620 orchard was a bit of an oddball. It had the Model 620 engine and driveline components and all the options, but in other respects it was a continuation of the AO and 60 orchard series. Deere continued production of the 620 orchard to the end of the two-cylinder era in 1960 even though it reintroduced the 20 series as the 30 series in 1958.

A fully restored LP version of the Model 620 standard that was built in 1957. Records indicate that only 37 were built. *John Detmer*

The Model 630, in any version, is a collector's item. This is a gas-burning row-crop version in Manitoba that has been nicely restored. *John Dietz*

This Model 630 row-crop tractor is the rare LP version. It was a project completed at Early Iron Restoration in Texas. *Kenny Earman*

Pretty as a postcard! This Model 630 standard, gas-burning model was built in 1959 and lives in Ohio. *Dave Hadam*

As a group, the 20 and 30 series are more sought after by today's collectors. These were the green and yellow tractors that Dad used when the baby boomers were going off to grade school, and they were the last of Deere's two-cylinder tractor production in North America. They were and are good tractors. Many are still in use as chore tractors on today's small farms and too busy at real work to be available for the collector market.

Collectors need to be aware that Deere provided early and late versions of the 620, basically a year apart. The early 620 had a spoke steering wheel (as did the Model 60), plus a green dash and black generator. The late 620 had a molded all-plastic steering wheel, black dash, green generator, and molded all-plastic steering wheel. Of the two, the late 620, or black dash 620, is more desirable.

Replacement decals, gauges, and breathers are available for most two-cylinder tractors. *John Dietz*

Although it wasn't separately tested at Nebraska, the late 620 had more engine speed and a bit more horsepower.

Generally, the Model 620 is collectable but not particularly pricey. The value trend has been upward, though not clearly defined. About 70 percent of 100-odd sales records in the past decade are in the range of $2,000 to $4,000. At the high end, a 620 LP gas Hi-Crop sold for $90,000 at an Indiana auction in September 2003, about three months after an exceptional all-fuel Hi-Crop sold in Minnesota for $80,000.

Model 620 Buyers' Guide

"A sleeper? Probably the 620 standard would be one to pay attention to, especially one with a three-point. That was an option and there's no production records on it. To find a 620 or a 630 standard with a three-point is a bit of an eye-catcher. They're both very good tractors to have."
— Albert Ulrich, Renaissance Tractor, Chehalis, Washington

"Ron Coy had a 620 all-fuel Hi-Crop. I think there were three of those made and two were exported. That tractor, at the collector's center, brought $175,000."

— Gary Uken, Uken Tractor Restoration, Titonka, Iowa

Model 630

The Model 630 was one of seven 30 series tractors introduced by Deere & Company for 1959–1960 and was the successor to the Model 620. The row-crop version was offered alongside a 630 standard and 630 Hi-Crop. Excluding tractors made in Mexico, total production of all versions of the Model 630 came to slightly more than 18,000. Nearly 15,300 were the row-crop version with gasoline engines. Many of the remaining variations are rare to very rare. Rarest of the group is the 630 Hi-Crop. Only 19 were built, including 11 gasoline, 5 all-fuel, and 3 LP gas.

The 630 marked, with style and grace, the end of a production era dating back 25 years to the Model A. Internally, the engine and powertrain were nearly identical to the 620. In fact, it was never sent to the Nebraska Tractor Test Laboratory. For performance specifications, the results from the 1956 test for the 620 were used for the 630. However, it was quite a different tractor than the 620 for the operator and for today's collector.

Deere improved the paint scheme for the 30 series, including the 630. It removed the horizontal green rib at the bottom of the hood, letting the yellow bleed down and across in a sweeping, simpler, eye-appealing form that required fewer creases and bends on the assembly line. The steering shaft was hidden underneath the hood. The traditional round-pipe muffler was replaced with a new oval muffler that produced a quieter exhaust.

Operationally, the slanted steering wheel was at a more comfortable angle for the operator. The instrument panel also was redesigned with a two-tier approach that presented all the vital operating information on the angled upper tier. The starter pedal on the floor had been replaced with a push-button linked to a new solenoid mounted on the starter. The brake pedals were larger and easier to engage while wearing oversized overshoes. New flat-top fenders were offered, complete with a convenient handgrip and more protection for the operator. On the flat-top fenders, a farmer could mount four 12-volt lights and a radio.

The combination of these changes produced a very attractive tractor, then as a general-purpose tractor for real farm chores and now, nearly 50 years later, as a true collectors' item. A 630 Hi-Crop with gas engine, 1 of only 11 that were built, sold for $141,000 at a huge John Deere collectors' auction at the new John Deere Museum in Moline, Illinois, on August 8, 2000. It wasn't a fluke; another 630 Hi-Crop sold in 2003 for $116,000.

Taking out the exceptionally priced tractors, the normal range has been around $3,000 to $5,000 over the last decade for the Model 630s. The better prices in 2005 were $5,500 and upwards.

Model 630 Buyers' Guide

"If you're wanting the best value right now, it probably would be the 60. You wouldn't have a lot of money in it. If you're wanting the most resale value at the moment, it would be in the 30 series. They're hot right now; people just want that model."
— Kenny Earman, Early Iron Restoration, Mt. Pleasant, Texas

"You can find an unstyled A or a late styled A in decent running condition for $2,500 to $3,000. If you went with a mainstream 60 with a tricycle front end in just usable condition, that's a $2,500 tractor. If you did a 620 in pretty much the same condition, now you're into a $3,000 to $3,500 tractor. The 630 is probably $500 more, easily, in the same condition and configuration."
— Terry Robison, R .N. Johnson, Inc., Walpole, New Hampshire

"I can remember the first tractor bringing $20,000 or $30,000 or $50,000 and I thought, it's got to stop. Well, it hasn't stopped yet. I think, though, that the two-cylinder stuff will run its cycle just like the Model A and Model T Fords."
— Ron Jungmeyer, Jungmeyer Tractor Restoration Service, Russellville, Missouri

This pan seat provided spring and ventilation for long days in the field. *John Dietz*

Six types of cast rear wheels were provided for unstyled AR tractors. This one is ventilated with 18 holes! *John Dietz*

Production and Ratings

Model	Variant	Fuel	Model Years	Number Produced	Stars
A	Unstyled	Gas	1933-1938	65,031	*
A	Styled	All-Fuel	1939-1947	97,765	*
A	Late	Gas	1947-1952	90,025	*
A	Late	All-Fuel	1947-1952	16,015	*
A	H	Gas	1947-1952	246	****
A	H	All-Fuel	1947-1952	181	****
AN	Unstyled	Gas	1933-1938	591	***
AN	Styled	Gas	1939-1947	3,083	**
AN	H	Gas	1933-1938	26	*****
AN	Styled H	All-Fuel	1939-1947	236	****
AN	Late	Gas	1947-1952	4,011	**
AN	Late	All-Fuel	1947-1952	1,212	**
AO	Unstyled	Gas	1935-1949	2,686	**
AO	Late	All-Fuel	1949-1953	733	***
AO	S	Gas	1937-1941	820	***
AR	Unstyled	All-Fuel	1935-1949	17,394	*
AR	Late	Gas	1949-1953	9,900	*
AR	Late	All-Fuel	1949-1953	520	***
AW	Unstyled	Gas	1933-1938	303	****
AW	H	Gas	1933-1938	27	*****
AW	Styled	Gas	1939-1947	1,849	**
AW	Styled H	Gas	1939-1947	361	****
AW	Late	Gas	1947-1952	4,314	**
AW	Late	All-Fuel	1947-1952	1,961	**
60		Gas	1953-1956	48,916	*
60		All-Fuel	1953-1956	4,443	**
60		LP	1953-1956	3,807	**
60	H	All-Fuel	1952-1956	135	****
60	H	Gas	1952-1956	62	*****
60	H	LP	1953-1955	15	*****
60	O	All-Fuel	1953-1957	530	***
60	O	Gas	1953-1956	297	****
60	O	LP	1953-1957	45	*****
60	S High Seat	Gas	1954-1956	676	***
60	S High Seat	All-Fuel	1954-1956	209	****
60	S High Seat	LP	1954-1956	26	*****
60	S Low Seat	Gas	1953-1954	1,748	**
60	S Low Seat	All-Fuel	1953-1954	196	****
620		Gas	1956-1958	18,075	*
620		LP	1956-1958	2,520	**
620		All-Fuel	1956-1958	475	****
620	H	Gas	1956-1958	24	*****
620	H	LP	1956-1958	8	*****
620	O	Gas	1957-1960	427	****

Model	Variant	Fuel	Model Years	Number Produced	Stars
620	O	All-Fuel	1957-1960	202	****
620	O	LP	1957-1960	92	*****
620	S	Gas	1956-1957	920	***
620	S	LP	1956-1957	37	*****
620	S	All-Fuel	1956-1957	31	*****
630		Gas	1958-1960	15,254	*
630		LP	1958-1960	1,876	**
630		All-Fuel	1958-1960	181	****
630	H	Gas	1958-1960	11	*****
630	H	All-fuel	1958-1960	5	*****
630	H	LP	1958-1960	3	*****
630	S	Gas	1958-1960	706	***
630	S	All-Fuel	1958-1960	23	*****
630	S	LP	1958-1960	16	*****

Specifications

Model	A	60	620/630RC
Base price (1st year)	$1,175	$2,550	$3,200/$3,300
Width (in)	86	86.62	86.62
Height to radiator (in)	60	65.62	88.12
Length (in)	124	139	135.25
Weight (in)	3,525	5,300	5,858
Front tires/wheels (in)	24x4	6x16	6x16
Rear tires/wheels (in)	50x6	11-38	12.5-38
Fuel capacity (gal)	14	20.5	22.25
Coolant capacity (qt)	8	8.25	6.5
Gears forward/reverse	4/1	6/1	6/1

Engine / Power Data

	A Early	A Early	A Styled	A Late	AR Late
Fuel	Gas	All Fuel	All Fuel	Gas	Gas
Nebraska Test No.	222	378	335	384	429
Nebraska Test year	4/9/1934	10/27/1941	11/13/1939	6/7/1947	10/11/1949
Rated rpm	1,150	975	975	975	975
Bore and stroke (in)	4.25x5.25	5.5x6.75	5.5x6.75	5.6x6.75	5.6x6.75
Belt/PTO horsepower	16.01	30.33	29.59	38.02	39.1
Drawbar horsepower	11.84	26.52	26.2	34.14	34.9
Maximum pull (lb)	1,728	4,248	4,110	4,045	4,431
Shipping weight (lb)	3,275	6,350	6,410	6,574	7,367

	60*	60	620*	620
Fuel	Gas	LP	Gas	LP
Nebraska Test No.	472	513	598	591
Nebraska Test year	—/1952	11/6/53	10/10/56	10/6/56
Rated rpm	975	975	1,125	1,125
Bore and stroke (in)	5.5x6.75	5.5x6.75	5.5x6.37	5.5x6.37
Belt/PTO horsepower	41.6	42.2	48.68	50.34
Drawbar horsepower	36.9	38.1	44.16	45.78
Maximum pull (lb)	4,372	5,352	6,122	5,920
Shipping weight (lb)	7,413	7,609	8,655	8,769

*Note: A third Nebraska Test was done on both a 60 and 620 engine fueled with tractor fuel

Ratings
Collector's 5-Star LP Gas Editions

Model	Rating
630H	3
60H	15
630S	16
60S	26
600	45
60W	60

Parts Prices

MODEL	A		60		620		630	
	Low	High	Low	High	Low	High	Low	High
Air cleaner assembly	70				270		342	
Air cleaner intake stack	66	103			52	66	52	66
Amp gauge	20	70	20	28	20	28	20	28
Battery box/cover	50	195	90	120	90	120	90	120
Battery cable (set)	26	38						
Block	180							
Camshaft	45	146			227		227	
Carburetor	275	543	260	523	260	543	260	429
Carburetor float	23	36	25	28	25	28	25	28
Carburetor kit	17	30	20	61	20	61	20	61
Clutch drive disc	125	159	137	149	132	180	132	180
Clutch pulley cover	30	50	39	50	26	50	26	50
Clutch slider disc	56		56		56		56	
Connecting rod	60	194	135	144	115	124	115	
Crankshaft					556			
Cylinder head	375	455	421				495	
Dash	25							
Distributor	209	283	190	283	190	205	190	205
Distributor cap	30	55	15	30	17		17	
Exhaust manifold	139							
Exhaust pipe	25	132	24	132	24	132	24	132
Fender	129	217	129	164	129	200	129	200
Flywheel cover	150							
Fuel tank	60	100						
Generator	100	179	125	179	125	179	125	179
Grille screen	17	89	35	89	35	65	35	65
Grille with screen	340							
Headlight assembly	37	75	37	67	49	64	57	64
Magneto	160	375	310					
Manifold (intake & exhaust)	150	240	160	210	160	210	160	210
Muffler	25	62	25	62	23	56	39	56
Overhaul kit (piston, rings, etc.)	369	559	375	610	475	806	475	806
Pan seat	35	75						
Piston	60							
Piston rings	135		135		135		135	

MODEL	A		60		620		630	
	Low	High	Low	High	Low	High	Low	High
PTO shield	60	75	60	123	75	146	75	146
Radiator	243	316	316		316		316	
Radiator cap	19	90	13	25	6	15	5	15
Radiator core	142	315	128	315	128	315	128	315
Seat cushion (bottom)	28	50	28	50	28	60	28	60
Sediment bowl	24	45	18	24	18	24	18	24
Spark plug wires (set)	11	16	11	13	11	13	11	13
Starter	210	399	240	405	320	528	399	528
Starter drive assembly	25	43	34	43				
Steering wheel	44	75	44	65	49	140	49	140
Three-point hitch	410	693	410	693	325	647	325	647
Toolbox	30	50	37	45	37	45	37	40
Voltage regulator	36	52	36	52	37	52	37	52
Water pump	97	181	97	181	97	181	97	181
Weight, front			167		167		167	
Wheel bearings	69		69		69		69	
Wheel weights (405-lb set)			375		375		375	

Average Price at Auction

Model	A	60	620	630
1996–1997	$1,448	$2,329	$2,498	$4,223
2004–2005	$1,958	$2,295	$3,352	$6,313

Auction High Price

	A	60	620	630
1996	$3,750	$5,400	$4,000	$7,100
2005	$7,800	$57,000	$90,000	$116,000

Average Sale Value 1995 to 2010 (Actual and Projected)

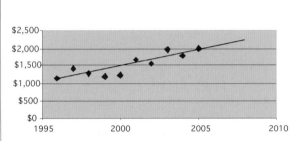

Model A: *1934-1952*

Machinery Pete: Average Sale Value, 309 Auctions

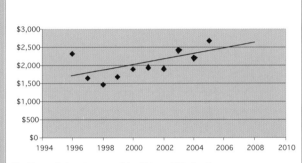

Model 60: *1952-1956*

Machinery Pete: Average Sale Value, 171 Auctions

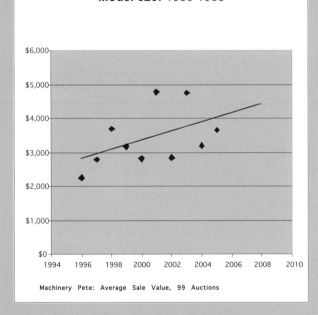

Model 620: *1956-1958*

Machinery Pete: Average Sale Value, 99 Auctions

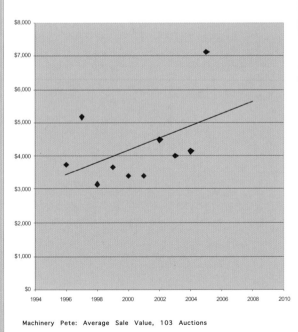

Model 630: *1958-1960*

Machinery Pete: Average Sale Value, 103 Auctions

Model A Anecdotes

"For a starter tractor I'd go with an old Model A, preferably a late A. There was a change in engine design in that series, and my preference is above the 584000 serial number because it was a little bit better engine design. The older the A, the harder it will be to find good parts. If you want an easy tractor to find parts for, and [have a] low budget to make yourself a nice old John Deere at minimum cost, you probably want to get a late A, made 1945 to 1953, even a real late one with a water pump.

"With those, if you engage the clutch you can pretty much feel what's been going on with the tractor. The clutch always required a bit of maintenance, and if it isn't quite right, it's probably just the tip of the iceberg.

"Like any tractor, if you want to get a feel for wear, look for wear around the bushing where the steering shaft is supported through the tower on top of the transmission. Look at the brake pedals to see how much the tread has been worn and think about where it's been used. If the fields are long and the tractor didn't make a lot of corners, it could have tons of time on without much wear on the steering bushings. The drawbar eye is another place to look. If the eye is about to go through the end of the drawbar, you know the thing has a few hours of seat time on it. Crankshaft end play is critical, but I don't find much problem with that on gas tractors compared to diesel tractors.

"Probably the biggest hidden expense you hit on a late A is a cracked block. Those late A blocks had a similar problem to the 60, though not quite as much. Regarding the block, look for signs of some freeze cracking and some welding that's patched it up. Other than that, if you've got loose clutch hubs or flywheel problems, you really know that just by checking it visually.

"Bumps and bruises on the front end? They're not too bad a problem; people are making reproduction grilles and screens, all kinds of good stuff. A guy in Kentucky is stamping out some new grille screens for those tractors and doing a very nice job, really production work.

"Restored in a set, those specialty tractors made in the late 1930s make a nice collection. If you start getting into that, you better have a good source of information on what needs doing and know where you're going to dig up parts and pieces, especially spoke wheels.

"The person who wants a spoke-wheel tractor, in any model, really needs to do his research. You could write a small resource book just on the options between steel and rubber and spokes and aftermarket wheels and specialty wheels. There were several applications of steel wheels, and they omitted higher gears for the steel wheels. If you find a Model A on rubber that is short a couple gears at the top end, that tractor probably was built for steel wheels and changed over. To find spoke wheels, head for a dry climate. With the moisture we have, there's none left around here, round or flat. Some guys do a pretty decent job with spoke-wheel reproductions, but you're probably going to pay $700 to $1,000 apiece.

"Whenever you get into unstyled tractors, especially the early row-crop tractors, you want to restore those characters to factory authenticity, what they were when they left the factory."

—Comments from Albert Ulrich, Renaissance Tractor, Chehalis, Washington

Only 99 Model GP tractors were manufactured in 1928 before Deere introduced the General Purpose (GP) tractor. A few of these tractors have been restored. *Bruce Keller*

This family of two-cylinder tractors emerged just before the Great Depression and continued through five model names to the end of the era in 1960. It may have had the best of the crop, as well as the worst. Essentially, this was the smallest of the general-purpose, basic row-crop tractors built at Waterloo. It came along after the Waterloo Boy and the initial success of the big Model D. This was Deere's replacement for a couple of teams of horses on the family farm in middle America and it worked very well. More than 400,000 units were built in this family of tractors. Collectors will find about 50 model variations in the family, and that's without testing out the different choices in wheels! The most common of these tractors in good-running condition can be found at country auctions, somewhere, every year. The auction value, not personal value, of one of these in good-running condition probably is around $2,000, give or take a thousand. On the other hand, some are very valuable. The highest recorded value at auction for a production model in this family through 2005 seems to be $35,000 for a Model C. It sold in Indiana in 1998 and was described as in poor condition but is one of only three known to exist at the time. One of the highest prices ever paid for a two-cylinder tractor also is associated with this family. Approximately $175,000 was paid for a rusty, original experimental tractor that was an ancestor to the entire John Deere General Purpose row-crop tractor production.

Model C

Deere & Company had enjoyed success with the Waterloo Boy and Model D. These machines had the brute power to plow a field or operate a threshing machine, but for the precision work, farms still needed teams of horses to pull planters and cultivators. With the Roaring 1920s in full throttle, it wasn't long before engineers and inventors had another traction machine for North American farmers. Deere's Model C row-crop tractor was introduced in 1927. It was improved for the 1928 model year and renamed the Model GP. Deere built fewer than 250 of these initial row-crop tractors. For collectors, they're exceptionally rare and valuable. Machinery Pete, a Minneapolis-based service, has been collecting auction sales data on all types of farm equipment since 1996. It has a growing network of contributors, currently located in 28 states. It is a key source of information on relative sales values for this book. During the 10 years ending in January 2006, only one Model C sale is recorded among approximately 2,250 auction sales records for John Deere two-cylinder tractors built through 1960. That tractor sold in southeast Indiana on December 5, 1998, for $35,000 in poor condition. It was described as "one of only three C's known to exist."

Deere designed the Model C during the 1920s. The company wanted a tractor that could straddle one row while planting or cultivating three rows. Competitors already were building a two-row tractor. In a comprehensive book, *The John Deere Unstyled Letter Series*, historian J. R. Hobbs has written of the Model C:

"Such a machine would have little side draft while pulling a two-bottom plow and would be smaller, more compact, and cheaper to build, while offering 50 percent more capacity than a two row machine."[4]

Two major developments occurred as Deere engineers worked on the row-crop concept. At the front, they developed a more precise steering system. They tested both one- and two-piece steering shafts. They also worked on power transfer and developing four sources of power for various operations.

These were available for the later Model C, which amounted to almost 100 tractors.

The revolutionary four-power system had the traditional drawbar and belt pulley. It also had a PTO and Power Lift mechanism. The PTO and Power Lift were a single unit engineered to provide power to either the front or the rear of the tractor. The PTO shaft essentially pointed both directions. The Power Lift assembly was attached and could raise or lower an implement at either end of the tractor without the aid of levers, springs, and muscle power. In fact, when the GP series replaced the Model C, Deere provided front-mounted cultivators operated by the Power Lift.

The company built 25 experimental all-crop tractors for field testing by farmers in March and April 1927. The assembly line built a second set of about 100 tractors starting in late 1917 and a third and final set ending in April 1928. The four-power feature was on the third set. After more improvements, Deere went into full production of its general purpose Model GP tractor for row-crops in August 1928.

The Model C is one of the most sought after of the entire John Deere two-cylinder tractor collection for good reason.

Only a handful were produced, and that's now more than 75 years ago. There are literally tens of thousands of enthusiasts and thousands more serious collectors who would love to own a Model C. Most of the Model C family stayed within one or two states' distance of the factory, but a few did go to New England, the South, and the West Coast. Most, if not all, of the Model C tractors were equipped with a wooden steering wheel and a pogo stick type of suspension for the seat. All were on steel wheels with round spokes, front and rear. However, a lost Model C may or may not have the standard 60-inch-wide front end. It is known that a few Model C tricycles did exist. The tricycle configuration was being tested at the same time.

Model C Buyers' Guide

"I just think the unstyled tractors will always be in demand because they were the first. If I dream John Deere at night, it's got spoke wheels on it." — Larry Baker, Clarkrange, Tennessee

"Collectors are fixing up just about anything that's salvageable and it's making it tougher to find parts. There's not a lot of engine reproduction parts available, other than piston rings stuff. If you buy one, you're going to have to rely on a

A ground-up view shows the two-way PTO system below the flywheel of the Model C.
Bruce Keller

Detail view of the engine and exhaust on the Model C. Note the exhaust elbow that points downward and the low-riding air cleaner.
Bruce Keller

The Model GP was produced from 1928 through 1935 in four variations—standard, orchard, wide tread, and potato. This 1930 GP has a standard tread and is shown at Rough and Tumble in Kinzers, Pennsylvania. *Jacob Merriwether*

A later 1935 Model GP is fully restored and carries the original GP tractor sweep rake. *Bruce Keller*

A 1930 Model GP is displayed at the Austin Museum in Manitoba with an older restoration. *John Dietz*

supplier, and that may take some calling around." — John Shephard, Shephard's 2-Cylinder, Downing, Wisconsin

Model GP

Collectors and old-tractor enthusiasts want to take note of the GP family of row-crop tractors. In eight short years, Deere produced enough variations on this model to generate a very large collection, or a small book. The GP was a work in progress rather than a great tractor. It had many faults that collectors need to respect today. The GP family also has several variations and subgroups. Variations included the GP wide tread, GP potato, and GP orchard. Each of these subgroups had several wheel combinations. Combined total production was about 34,500, which is relatively small when compared to production runs of more than 300,000 for more refined row-crop tractors that Deere produced in the mid-1930s.

Waterloo built nearly two-thirds of the GPs in just two years, 1929 and 1930. Production sank to less than 170 in 1933. It picked up in 1934, but ended completely in 1935.

John Deere's first row-crop tractor was easy to distinguish from the Model D because it had a frame in front to hold the wheels while providing better steering control. On the Model D, the front axle was attached directly to the engine block. This standard tread front-wheel configuration was built through 1935, but it wasn't the only one. A few GPs were made with the tricycle configuration. These gave a three-point ride with the narrowly spaced front wheels riding in the center furrow, and the rear wheels could ride in outside furrows. In the next decade, this became the most popular tractor configuration.

This beautiful Model GP orchard has been fully restored. These models are low and streamlined. This tractor has cast disc front wheels to avoid tangles with branches. *Bruce Keller*

This early 1933 Model GP wide tread with straight-across, over-top steering is one of 440 that were built. This has rare, round-spoke rear wheels with attached extension wheels. *Eddie Campbell*

A rare potato version of the Model GP. This is the second one, which was built in 1929. The wheels are narrower than on a standard GP. The front wheels are vertical compared to the camber on row-crop tractors. *Bruce Keller*

Early GP models coming off the 1928 assembly line broke new ground in several ways. It was the first tractor that offered four sources of power—belt, drawbar, power take-off, and the new Power Lift. The L-shaped flathead engine generated less horsepower on the GP than it had on the Model C and was discontinued after 1935. At only 20 to 22 horsepower, it struggled with the basic intent of the tractor: planting and cultivating on three rows. Tractor breakdowns were frequent. For instance, the air intake plugged easily

until Deere corrected the problem with a vertical air intake stack in 1929.

One interesting variation on the 1930 GP standard is known as the crossover standard. This was a set of tractors with a larger, 6-inch engine bore, and improved intake/ exhaust system. Most were shipped to Manitoba and Ontario, Canada. Historian J. R. Hobbs writes of these, "... this is one instance where no GP parts book known to be published will tell you anything about these tractors. . . . The discovery of some early service

This showroom is part of a 1950s-style John Deere dealership replica built to house the collections of partners Steve Kidd and Robert Kraehling in southwest Ontario. The tractor in the foreground is a pristine Model GP wide tread. *Gerry Dubrick*

bulletins in the late 1980s, as well as the recovery of some of the tractors themselves, proves without a shadow of a doubt that these critters were actually built. Very few of these 68 tractors are known to exist today."[5]

The improved engine, with its 6-inch bore and new intake/exhaust system, was standard for the next four years, 1931 to 1935. Collectors know them as the Big Bore GP as opposed to the Small Bore GP. The engine now had cleaner air. It also received a new oil filter that provided better lubrication. There were changes in the main bearings, governor, steering, final drives, and main case. It also had heavier front and rear wheels.

Halfway through the 1931 production, Deere made further changes. It increased cooling capacity with a larger radiator core and brought in a new insulated fuel tank.

Air-filled rubber tires were offered for the first time in late 1932 as an option on the GP. For industrial use, hard rubber tires had been an option since the 1920s. It took extensive testing and marketing, but eventually Firestone Rubber & Tire Co. showed that rubber offered better traction than steel, as well as a more comfortable ride.

By 1934, the GP was a much better tractor and the economy was looking a little better. Production climbed to 1,250 units. For that year, the GP received a new carburetor, the DLTX 5, which replaced the finicky Ensign K carburetor.

Even as production was ending for 1935, Deere made one further change that created another subgroup of the Big Bore GP series. The 1935 models got a new Vortox oil bath air cleaner. Production that year was about 230 tractors; a very limited edition.

The last GP rolled off the assembly line in March 1935, making way for what became a stunning success and one of the most popular Deere two-cylinder tractors ever.

One note about wheels: According to the records now residing with the Two-Cylinder® Club, 21 separate parts numbers exist for GP standard wheels, front and rear. The basic options include flat or round spokes on steel wheels, round-spoke wheels for hard rubber tires, and round-spoke wheels for pneumatic tires. Other options were a flat steel wheel with flat spokes (in two sizes), a flat-spoke skeleton wheel (in two sizes), an extension wheel for hard rubber, and a wheel with an offset hub for a beam axle.

At auction, the GP is showing up more frequently and is increasing in value. Typical auction values in 2005 were $4,000 to $6,000.

In the Model B family of Deere two-cylinder tractors, this is Adam all-fuel, the first production unit. It was built on October 2, 1934. It has the skeleton steel wheels with even-spaced lugs on the rear and cast front Texas wheels. *Bruce Keller*

GPWT

The GP Wide Tread (GPWT) was authorized in 1929, but a few were built earlier. Fourteen had been built in 1928, shortly after GP production began, and others were built in early 1929 before the official authorization. There were 5,000 wide treads built before the series was cancelled in 1933. In just four years of production, the GPWT had 12 wheel options and three different carburetors.

The GPWT was longer, wider, and taller than the GP, although it had the same engine and transmission. It was 2 inches taller, 5 inches longer, had a 86-inch-wide tread at the back compared to 60 inches on the GP. The late overhead steer version of the GPWT (1932–1933) was 17 inches longer than the GP. Today GPWT owners can have trouble finding a trailer that's able to hold a tractor nearly 11 feet long and more than 7 feet wide.

This tractor was built for three-row work but could be used for two- or four-row operations, like planting or cultivating, working up to 45 acres a day when equipped with four-row implements and Power Lift. The 1929 GPWT had issues that affected the production life. The air cleaner was prone to plugging until a vertical air stack was adopted toward the end of

1929. A revised cylinder head was provided in 1930 as a temporary fix for problems with the original water-injected flathead engine. Later that year, a new 6-inch-bore engine was fitted, along with a new intake and exhaust manifold and a new carburetor. The 1931 model changes included a new location for the air cleaner, introduction of an oil filter to prolong engine productivity, and an improved exhaust system that made life for the operator a lot more comfortable. It was improved so much that the Union of Soviet Socialist Republics (USSR) ordered the delivery of 27 units in 1931.

Further changes in mid-1932 production led to a new nickname, the overhead steer GPWT. The steering box was combined with the front pedestal that was now mounted on the front of the tractor chassis, and the front wheels had casters that eliminated whip when changing rows. Operator visibility and comfort were much improved with a series of changes. The operator was sitting about a foot forward and 10 inches higher. Production on these was slow. Waterloo built only about 270 improved GPWT tractors in 1932 and about 150 more in 1933.

The GPWT has emerged strongly in the past 10 to 15 years as a collector's item. It currently has the highest value in the GP series. A restored GPWT with overhead steer sold for $26,000 in a 2005 auction, as it was one of only 417 that were built.

A separate version of the GP for potato growers was delivered in 1930. The GP potato special had been approved by Deere in November 1929. These had a 68-inch tread suited to two 34-inch potato rows instead of the standard 74-inch tread for a GPWT. The GP potato special also had a new serial plate, starting at P-5000. There were two production runs, each lasting about four weeks, in 1939. Serial number P-5202 was the last potato special unit. Most were sent to New York, Maine, and eastern Canada. It's interesting to note that these serial number tags were the only ones Deere ever produced that began and ended with only four digits.

A GP orchard edition was authorized in February 1931. It had a four-year run and more than 700 were built. The GPO had a low, streamlined profile for moving under branches and around tight corners. Even the operator's seat was lower. At 49 inches tall, it was the lowest two-cylinder production tractor ever built by Deere. The GPO benefited from many changes already in place for the GP family. The carburetor was upgraded about midway in production. Deere offered three wheel options for the front and three for the rear. It had an extensive list of options, such as cast disc front wheels, a concave steel plate that kept low branches from being caught in wheel spokes, and citrus fenders. It proved to be a good, reliable tractor and many have survived. Any GPO that can be found today can be considered a rare tractor and worthy of restoration. They were shipped to orchards all over the United States and Canada.

Model GP Buyers' Guide

"When I started, nobody cared about GPs. First, they [Deere] never said they made them. Then, the last 8 or 10 years, everybody's got real excited about them. Particularly, the GPs really come on strong here the last three or four years. I paid $16,000 for the last GP I bought and it was a bucket of bolts.

"They made 711 of the GPO and 7,000 have survived! About anybody who's a very serious collector has a GPO. They had a very high survivability. Neighbors and I have taken five out of the woods up here. They sold a lot of them right here and a lot in Michigan.

"The GP small-bores are much more prevalent and, generally speaking, are less costly than the big-bores. The small-bore tractors that are in restorable condition, with all the parts, not a nightmare, probably running, will go for anywhere from $3,000 to $5,000. The big-bores, in the same condition, usually go for $4,000 to $6,000.

"The GP was never a well-designed tractor. By the time they corrected all the problems in 1931, the model had a pretty bad name. It's a real goofball tractor. The exhaust and intake are on the same side. The gas tank on the early ones does not have insulation and it sits right on top of the exhaust manifold so the fuel will boil. It's got some real stupid things, and they're very prone to fire.

"If you had a bad carb, bad mag, and not a handy tractor, that's the reason I think a lot of those survived. They were too new for scrap but didn't run worth crap so they didn't have a chance to wear them out.

"In 1934, 80 percent of tractors were shipped with steel (wheels) and 20 percent with rubber. By 1937, that number had flipped, thanks to Harvey Firestone showing how pneumatic tires will increase the traction. The GPs that came out on round-spoke rubber were quite rare in production, but a lot have survived. In the 1950s and 1960s, you could use rubber where you couldn't go down the roads with cleats. When I was a kid, they used to have signs that said, 'No Lugs Allowed' on the road, and that was for tractors."

— Bart Cushing, Walpole, New Hampshire

"I've been doing carburetors since 1957. I got interested in the GP about 1987 while I was at the first Two-Cylinder Expo at the Waterloo airport. I started going to auctions, looking for GPs and eventually I got into the GP restoration business. During the early days of my business, if you had a John Deere A and a GP in similar general condition, side by side at an auction, the A would always bring maybe two or three times as much as a GP. Now, it's just the other way around. It's supply and demand.

"The rarest of the GP series is obviously the C, and next in line would be the Model P, for potato. At the 2005 Collector's Centre auction at Moline, a Model P in pretty bad condition sold for $28,000 and it did not have the correct wheels on it. It's in the [restoration] process now at my Tractor Trauma Center. The only other one I know of sold for $46,000 four or five years ago, and it only ran; it was not a good restoration.

This is a 1935 four-bolt B row-crop tractor at a Rough and Tumble event in Pennsylvania. The Model 520 beside the B is a direct descendant of the B that was built about 20 years later. *Jacob Merriwether*

"I know of three GP tractors with Over-The-Top Steer that sold in the last two years. One sold for $26,000 and did not run, had incorrect wheels. Another one sold for about $18,000. The GP Wide Tread Side Steer crossover is, again, hard to find. Probably, if you found a rusty hulk, you'd be lucky if you could get it for $10,000 to $12,000.

"In 1935, they went to an oil bath air cleaner on the GP. I have seen just the air cleaner for a 1935 unit bring more than $2,000. So a decent 1935 GP is very desirable and worth quite a bit of money.

"Carburetors on the early GP were made by Jensen. There's three distinct, different styles and they're also very hard to find. The next one for the GP was the Marvo Schivler and it looked very similar to the early brass carburetor on the 1934–1935 A. It's a different number; it's got different features on it. I've heard of people having to pay $700 to get the correct late Marvo Schivler brass carburetor for a Big Bore GP."

— Cork Groth, Tractor Trauma Center, Eldredge, Iowa

"And the steering on the early Wide Tread, with the side steer, was a very poor steering. They tell me that in a year or two it got wore so bad you couldn't even cultivate and keep between the rows."

— Ron Jungmeyer, Jungmeyer Tractor Restoration Service, Russellville, Missouri

This unstyled but beautiful 1936 Model B row-crop tractor has round-spoke wheels for rubber tires and rare French and Hecht front wheels. *Kenny Earman*

One of the first styled B row-crop tractors is shown with an electric starter, lights, and front spokes. This is a 1939 model. *Eddie Campbell*

Watch Out

"Look at the final drives in both the small- and big-bore. The early final drives were shaped in almost a triangular form; the latter finals were shaped like an egg. The chains loosened up, and they'd go down and wear the case out on the final drives. A lot of times you buy an early tractor and think you've done really well and find out you've got later final drives on it.

"On the big-bore, the head is a problem. I can get a head repaired if it has not been welded. If you've got a GP with a smashed-up head that leaks like a sieve, that's already been welded, you can see $2,000 to $3,000 to go get another head if you can find it. That amount is not uncommon; I've spent it.

"The GP had Fairbanks Morse magnetos that had the John Deere name on the cap. They ran terrible and almost everybody replaced them. They're very expensive to rebuild, but they're extremely valuable today."

— Bart Cushing, Walpole, New Hampshire

"Another thing on the GP is the fuel tank. They didn't make nearly as many GPs as As and Bs, and it's virtually impossible to find a good used fuel tank for a GP.

"Look at is the steering arms, where they attach to the upright spindle. John Deere used a very, very fine spline on the steering spindle. The shaft is only 1½ inch diameter, and it has 48 splines. If the operator didn't keep the clamp bolts very tightly secured, the fine spline starts working and you wear the spline off. You'll find everything from a hole drilled from the top down with a peg pounded in, to a hole drilled all the way through with a bolt sticking through it, to somebody welding it or braising the steering arms to the top of the upright spindles.

"Another weakness on the GP was the rear axle housing. There are several different housings through the evolution of the GP. It's not unusual to see an early GP with dissimilar final drive housing because one of them broke. The reason it broke was that it was too weak to begin with. The reason they're dissimilar is they knew that problem and said if you're going to fix it, you may as well put this newer one on, and they won't match."

— Cork Groth, Tractor Trauma Center, Eldridge, Iowa

A 1950 late styled Model B in a prairie collection is nicely restored. This is a fine example of a Johnny Popper. *John Dietz*

A rare Model BN from 1935 is equipped with 28-inch spoke wheels. Deere advertised this as the B garden tractor and built only 24 of these for work in Arizona and California. *Bruce Keller*

Model B

The Model B was second only to the Model A as the most popular two-cylinder tractor that Deere & Company ever produced, but not by much. There may well be more Model B tractors available today than any other model discussed in this book. From 1934 through to the end of production in 1953, Deere built approximately 314,000 tractors in the Model B family, compared to just over 320,000 in the Model A family. Production peaked in 1937 at 21,248 Model B tractors and 24,080 Model A tractors. The little B weighed about 2,800 pounds, 1,000 pounds less than the Model A being built nearby, and 1,600 pounds less than the Model G that

was introduced that year. It also had less horsepower, but was ideal for tens of thousands of small farms across America.

General categories for the B family include unstyled, early styled (1939–1947), and late styled (1948–1953). Three unstyled variations of the Model B were the BN, BW, and BH. Production of these variations in 1937 included about 400 BN tractors, 88 BW tractors, and 10 BNH tractors. Most operated with the cheapest and lowest octane fuel, identified as distillate, and were promoted as an all-fuel tractor. A gasoline engine also was available; many of these still exist. As well, there were three purpose-built subsets that are each rare to extremely rare.

Parked in shade after the parade, this 1930 Model B orchard (right) is beside a later member of the two-cylinder family, a 1954 Model 60. *Jacob Merriwether*

A basic Model B row-crop tractor, not restored, is about as ideal a starter tractor as any collector can hope to find and shouldn't be too hard to find. The price will be, or should be, about as low as can be found for any John Deere two-cylinder tractor in comparable condition. Parts will almost always be readily available. The selection of good-quality reproduction parts is increasing every year. The size is about two-thirds as large as the Model A, which is small enough to fit nicely in a one-car garage or haul with a pickup. It probably will be a simple tractor to work on. It isn't hard to start. Once it's running, it probably won't quit until it's out of fuel.

Machinery Pete recorded approximately 350 Model B tractor sales at auction between 1996 and 2005. For all Model B tractors, the price trend at auction has risen from about $1,100 in 1996 to $1,900 at the end of 2005. Comparing averages for the year, the 1996 value was $1,400; the 2005 value was about $2,100. A high-end 1937 B on round spokes, with overhead steer, sold for $9,000 in a Minnesota auction in 2005.

Among the rare collectables, values are much higher. Records show that that six B orchard tractors sold in 2005 for an average of about $10,000 apiece. The BRs were selling at around $4,000 to $7,000. It seems hard to find a BWH or BWH-40 at auction. Winning bidders in the past five

This standard tread unstyled BR has seen some hard days as a mobile sawmill in Manitoba. *John Dietz*

Extended wide and high, this BWH is one of only 51 built in 1938. It also had a long frame. *Bruce Keller*

An autumn postcard from the Wisconsin woods: an unstyled 1938 Model BWH-40 beside a styled 1940 BWH-40 from Waterloo. *Bruce Keller*

years have been paying $60,000 to $80,000 for these very rare machines.

Unstyled B

The B was, in essence, a scaled-down Model A. It was commissioned in 1933 to be two-thirds the size, power, and weight of the Model A that was nearly ready for production. The first B came down the production line on October 2, 1934, and only 43 units later, Deere introduced its first variation.

Deere corrected a design flaw in February 1935. The front pedestal had been fastened to the main frame by only four bolts. Field work put too much stress on the four connecting points, which led to breakage. Deere gave the B a cast-iron front pedestal securely mounted with eight bolts and solved the problem. Today, the Four Bolt B is one of the most sought-after collector tractors. Deere had built just over 2,000 by that point. Most of the Four Bolt B pedestals eventually broke and were replaced with the eight-bolt version.

Within the Four Bolt group were subsets that are even rarer. Anyone owning a 1934 or early 1935 B should go to the serial number records held by the Two-Cylinder Club for detailed information. The very first had a brass-tag serial-number plate intended for the GP series, but bearing the B serial numbers. The first seat frames were a solid casting. This was upgraded twice in the late unstyled Model B tractor, first with a center hole in the casting. This seat frame was in use before the eight-bolt pedestal was introduced. The final seat frame had a reinforcing ring around the shaft to prevent it from breaking. The three types interchange but are distinctly different.

Another characteristic of the early unstyled B (and unstyled A) was a fuel cap located under the steering rod in the center of the hood. Most owners had to use an offset funnel to get fuel into the tank. On the dash, the early unstyled B also had an oil gauge as standard equipment. The temperature gauge was an option for a few years.

Deere offered a garden tractor variation, the BN, to the basic B. The BN was tall, wide at the back, and equipped with a single front nose wheel for vegetable growers to maneuver in very narrow rows. For looks or shape, it has been described as a 1930s version of a stealth bomber. Drivers had to be careful that when heading downhill they didn't hit a bump with the BN's single front wheel. Deere built 800 unstyled BNs. Only 24 early BNs were built prior to an important structural change in 1935. These were shipped to Arizona and California and are among the rarest of any model of John Deere tractor.

A second variation, the BW, was introduced in 1935. It had an adjustable wide front end. It was intended to provide more stability in narrow row-crops where growers wanted front

A nicely restored Model 50 is shown in the pothole country of southwestern Manitoba. *John Dietz*

The nose and grille of many Bs were banged up around the farm. If a grille needs to be replaced on your B, an original or reproduction grille shouldn't be hard to find. *John Dietz*

and rear wheels in the same track. About 250 unstyled BWs were built. A change to a better front-axle design made the first 25 of these especially collectable. On the 1936 assembly line, six models were designated as experimental. They were given special front and rear axle housings that could be narrowed to 40 inches with steel wheels. There are only three BW-40s known to survive.

Two more variations on the B appeared for growers in 1936 models. These were the smaller version of the Model A series standard tread tractors and were named the BR and BO. The B main case was modified to accept a different steering system. Many other changes were made with the end result a small and fairly popular version of the AR and AO. To adapt the BR to orchard requirements, the BO was provided with differential brakes for short turning, a lower air stack, and shields for the air stack, fuel, and gasoline filler caps. Improvements being adopted in other Deere tractors were picked up for the BR and BO.

The two models had several important changes in 1939. They were given a larger engine, which increased the displacement from 149 to 175 cubic inches. With a recalibrated carburetor and other minor revisions, the new BR and BO offered an important power boost. Late in the year, electric starting and electric lighting were offered as options. These two models were not restyled with the rest of the B family in 1939. Instead, they continued rolling off the assembly line through early 1947. Deere had built 6,400 BR tractors and nearly 5,100 BO tractors. Out of this group, Deere removed approximately 1,675 for conversion into crawler tractors by the Lindeman Power Equipment Company of Yakima, Washington. Instead of wheel assemblies, the BO main case rode on Lindeman's tracks and undercarriage.

Late in 1936 and early in 1937, some B series tractors were equipped with a modified radiator. The radiator curtain

The Model B was easy to drive and operate. The late B dash had white-faced gauges until near the end of production in 1952. *John Dietz*

There's a load of parts under this sheet metal. Most parts are available, but look over tractor parts carefully if they are for sale. *John Dietz*

A detail view of the throttle and radiator shutter controls on the steering column. If it's still original, be sure they're not seized up. *John Dietz*

assembly was replaced by radiator shutters, making it easier to control engine temperature.

Deere stretched the General Purpose Model B tractor frame in June 1937 by 5 inches, giving it the same wheelbase as the Model A. The new long-frame B series had a longer hood, steering shaft, fan shaft, gas tank intake, and exhaust pipe. The two types are known as short-frame and long-frame tractors. The easiest way to detect a long-frame B is by a quick look at the air horn on the carburetor. On a short-frame B, the air pipe makes a straight vertical join between the carburetor and air cleaner. On the long-frame unstyled B, it reaches horizontally about 5 inches and has an elbow to take it up to the air cleaner.

Late in 1937, Deere met requests for variations in the BN and BWH. Growers wanted a high-clearance version of the BN, so Deere added 2 inches of vertical clearance and called the new version a BNH. Rear tread width could be adjusted to 104 inches. Only 10 were built in 1937 and another 55 in 1938, prior to introduction of styling for the B family. The BWH was the wide-front version of the high-clearance line, providing more stability. Only 51 unstyled BWH models were produced in 1938.

One more variant, the BWH-40, was produced in 1938, but production numbers are unknown. It had a minimum tread width of 42⅝ inches and required fenders as standard equipment. It was available only with rubber tires. It was intended for crops grown in 20-inch rows on 40-inch beds, but could be spaced up to 80 inches wide. At least six exist.

Generally, a Model B could be ordered with wheel equipment to suit the owner. Rubber tires were available from the start. Wheels for rubber can be found with round spokes, flat

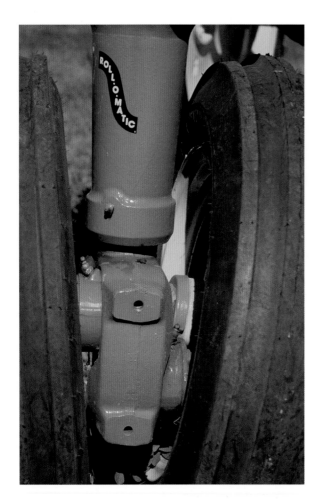

Roll-O-Matic knee-action suspension was introduced as an option on the 1947 Model B. *John Dietz*

spokes, and cast-iron centers. Flat steel rear wheels and steel front wheels with guide bands were standard. Spade lugs could be obtained in two sizes. There were specialty lugs (sand, button, cone), and for growers with sticky soil, the skeleton-style steel rear wheel could be used. A very rare option was a 1937 tip-toe-style steel rear wheel.

Note that the original parts for the John Deere unstyled B, especially engine parts, are becoming scarce.

Generally, a long-frame unstyled B in running condition today can be purchased at auction for around $2,000. Privately, you may pay more.

Styled B

New York industrial designer Henry Dreyfuss toured the Waterloo factory in 1936. When he returned to the Big Apple, he started sketching styling proposals for Deere & Co. In addition to styling, he had proposals for improving operator visibility, comfort, convenience, and safety. His ideas would filter through the tractor parade, starting with the Model B. The styled B was the first on the assembly line in July 1938 as a 1939 model. It was a big success. The Model B became the sales leader, displaced the Model A, and stayed there until the end of the 1946 model year.

Streamlined styling graced the sheet metal. Inside, the B was even better. It had more power and more torque, thanks to an increase in bore and stroke. The new B was available in a wide variety of configurations: the regular B tricycle model, the BN with a single front wheel, the BW with wide adjustable front axle, the BNH with single front wheel and high clearance, the BWH with wide adjustable front end and high clearance, and the BWH-40 with fenders and a special narrow-tread rear axle housing. The B line had a wide variety of wheel equipment options and a choice of factory-installed transmissions. Fenders and hydraulic Power Lift were optional.

Electric starting and electric lighting became available in 1940. Rubber tires were so popular by this point that the B on rubber was equipped with a new six-speed transmission and another increase in horsepower, thanks to an improved carburetor. For 1941 and later, the dash was changed.

The first system that could operate a remote hydraulic cylinder on a farm tractor was introduced by Deere in October 1945 on Model B tractors under the name Powr-Trol. Availability was very limited until the 1947 model year. It then was made available to retrofit earlier tractors.

Late B production began in February 1947 and ended with the 1952 model year. Production included approximately 96,000 with gas engines and 13,000 with all-fuel engines. Variations were reduced to three: the B, BN, and BW.

The late B was a greatly improved tractor over the early B. For power, it had a revised engine, known as the Cyclone. Engineers had placed an eyebrow next to the intake valve, inducing a swirl that kept the air-fuel mixture in suspension and enabled more power to be produced. Engine bore was

Watch Out

"Watch out for a noisy transmission and the hydraulic lift. The biggest problem I feel is the transmission gears. If you ran into something, that could be the end of the radiator. On many of them, the radiator's been patched and patched and patched. They've shoved stuff through both sides even. The PTO worked good, and the belt worked good. Otherwise, they weren't a problem." — Frank Baker, Clarkrange, Tennessee

"In the late styled B, the cluster gear in the transmission was the biggest thing. It got to making a lot of horsepower and the transmission started giving trouble. When they went to the six-speed and finally got that last power boost, it started playing on the transmission." — Frank Baker, Clarkrange, Tennessee

Model B. *John Dietz*

"I don't know that anybody is really making a gas tank yet for the unstyled B. That would be nice if somebody would start making unstyled gas tanks." — Frank Baker, Clarkrange, Tennessee

increased, giving the new engines 190 cubic inches, and engine speed was increased to 1,250 rpm.

A new six-speed transmission with a creeper gear and a single control lever also was introduced. Electric lighting and electric start became standard. A cushioned seat was introduced and controls were more convenient than ever.

At the front end, Deere introduced Roll-O-Matic, a new knee-action suspension system, on the 1947 Model B. The Roll-O-Matic system offered a smoother ride than a traditional narrow front end. It is similar to a semi-independent front suspension. When one wheel hit a bump, a gear forced the other wheel down to keep it in contact with the ground. This prevented the tractor from hopping, making it more comfortable, as well as easier to control and steer. Powr-Trol was now standard, and Power Lift was available. Other popular options included fenders and heavy cast rear wheels.

Once the late B series was introduced, only a few changes were required. The magneto was changed from a Wico C to a Wico X to a Wico XD. Due to popular demand, a two-piece front pedestal was offered, with or without

Roll-O-Matic. The rear axle housing was adjusted from round to square, and clamshell fenders replaced the earlier design. Due to the Korean War, copper was in short supply and the last B series tractors had steel radiator cores.

Model B Buyers' Guide

"Three years ago [2003] I had blocks and heads galore out here for mid-1940s and early 1950s Bs. Now I'm short of those parts for almost all models. Guys are starting to repair the fence row tractors and they need everything. A lot of times they'll put more money into them than probably the average value. As the Number series values increase, guys that wanted to work on the lower end of the dollars have been buying As and Bs and Ds to fix them up. Many times the best buy these days is a tractor that's repaired and ready to go.

"Parts for the 1939 and 1940 B are getting harder to find. John Deere styled that tractor and made some minor changes in the engine. Everything is pretty specific, so it's a little more difficult to find parts. The 1941 through 1946 B parts are plentiful in used and reproductions; the same with

On the 1950 late styled B tractors, clamshell-shaped fenders replaced the earlier design. They wouldn't plug with mud but they left the operator with less protection. *John Dietz*

the late styled B. It seems like there are enough parts out there to repair them.

"I get calls every day from guys looking for unstyled blocks and heads. We get calls from all over the United States and Canada looking for parts. Occasionally we've shipped to Australia, Ireland, Germany, [the] Netherlands. Five years ago I had never shipped overseas."

— John Shephard, Shephard's 2-Cylinder,
Downing, Wisconsin

"The long frame had no weaknesses that I know of. They were fairly durable. When they were wore out, if you had some

baling wire and a pair of pliers, you could still get another 10 or 12 years of service. They'd run in pretty sad condition and keep on running. A bad mag, probably, was the biggest problem. That probably kept it from running more than anything. Carburetors could be pretty full of crud and still keep on going. Valves could be awful weak and rings could be awful weak, but you'd just pour in oil and let 'em go. If you didn't have spark, you couldn't get 'em started.

"The Bs are getting more valuable. On a farm sale I've seen them bring $1,900 for one that was stuck. The easy-picking ones are gone. You still find them tucked away in a shed or something, but you won't see them sitting beside a shed or along the fence row on the highway. You won't see that anymore."

— Don Doeden, Cook, Nebraska

"Most BNs came with wide axles and farmers didn't like them because they were forever running into the side of the barn or a tree. Most of them set the wheel where they wanted it, took a torch, and cut off the axle ends. They were not a real popular tractor here and actually, they're not that popular with collectors. I've had a short-frame unstyled BN but they don't bring money. You don't see an AN bringing much, either. They may be undervalued.

"The unstyled B was a real liked tractor. It was cheap. It didn't burn much gas. Young sons and daughters could drive this tractor because it was light. It was easy to turn. It didn't compact the ground in your garden or vegetables. There were guys who farmed 40 acres with a John Deere B unstyled. They called it a mule because of the way it looked, and they'd do an acre every hour and a half.

"Older men like the BOs and BRs for the same reason a lot of them are buying the Ms. It's because of the trailer ramps. They don't have to do that center ramp for the tricycle front end. If you load it at home, load it at the show, and load it back home, that's three or four times you don't have to pick up a third ramp. If you're 70 years old, that may be a real thing."

— Frank Baker, Clarkrange, Tennessee

Model 50

The successor to the Model B, the Model 50, is a bit of an oddball for collectors. The average garden-variety John Deere

A 1957 Model 520 LP row-crop tractor in Kansas. *John Detmer*

Detail view of the adjustable-width front axle on a Model 50. *John Dietz*

50 is far harder to find than a Model B, and it's a far better tractor if you want to put a few working hours on it. For value, it's only a little more money than a Model B. Auction records indicate the Model 50 is selling for perhaps $500 more than a similar late styled B, but about half the price of its newer brother, the Model 520, and much less than Model 530. At auction, approximately 100 Model 50 tractor sales are recorded in the past 10 years. The trend in the rising value for a Model 50 is among the lowest in the entire two-cylinder Deere collection. The average auction value for the Model 50, over 10 years, has increased about one-third. The number of these tractors offered at auction has been increasing. In 2005, 20 sales of $500 value or more were noted in the Model 50 class. Combined average sales value for 35 tractors in 2004–2005 was approximately $2,600, with a range from $500 to $5,500.

The Model 50 is one member of a group known as the first Numbered series of John Deere two-cylinder tractors. The 50, 60, 70, and 80 replaced the B, A, G, and R tractor lines. The Model 40 was introduced about the same time and came out of the Dubuque factory. Rather than naming variations and building them at the factory, Deere provided five front-end choices and allowed dealerships to install whatever the buyer wanted. The front-end choices were single wheel, dual

wheels, Roll-O-Matic wheels, 38-inch tread, and adjustable-tread axles. The hi-crop version was not an option on the 50, but it was available for the 60 and 70. An optional extrawide rear-end axle also was available for the 50, 60, and 70.

The model years for the 50 are 1953 through 1956. The first five were built in July 1952 before the annual factory shutdown, and four of these were shipped to Deere's experimental department. Another 125 were built between August and October when a steel strike shut down production.

Gasoline and all-fuel engines were available from the start for the Model 50. A new dual carburetor was only offered for the gasoline version. In 1955, Deere began equipping a few of the engines to burn liquid propane, which never proved as popular, but eventually Deere sold more than 700 of these Model 50 tractors.

Deere never felt a need to provide variations on the Model 50 basic row-crop configuration. However, early in the 1954 production run, a two-piece convertible pedestal was made standard. It replaced a nonconvertible pedestal and allowed various front-end configurations to be made at the dealership or farm level.

Other changes in 1954 included a new Delco-Remy distributor and a conventional thermostat system to replace the new-but-troublesome thermostatically controlled shutter system.

The first integrated, factory-designed, power steering system for farm tractors was introduced on the Model 50 for the 1955 model year. Deere's system was a breakthrough and major advance in operator comfort and convenience.

The last production year, 1956, saw the addition of the 801 Traction-Trol three-point hitch on the Model 50. It replaced the 800 and 800A hitches.

Deere produced approximately 200 special editions for the Barber-Greene Company of Aurora, Illinois. Barber-Greene used the Model 50 as the power unit for its Model 550 windrow loader. Even the wheels of these units had a coat of Barber-Greene paint. They also had a special cast 28-inch rear wheel, and a single front wheel with a shorter yoke. They were built without a PTO or rockshaft. Ground speed in first gear was slashed 75 percent to aid in building windrows of snow, dirt, and other material.

Model 50 Buyers' Guide

"As far as today, the 50 doesn't sell real good but it's starting to get a little hotter. They're worth anywhere from $1,600 to $3,500 now. They're a good bargain. I think they're going to be a sleeper.

"I can take you to farmers that still have the 50 in the barn that they bought brand new, and it's ready to go. They are a tough little old tractor. They didn't have enough horsepower to tear up themselves. Most of the old guys really liked them.

"Everybody wants a B or a 50 at plow day cause they're light. You don't need a big truck. You can bring two on the same trailer with a ¾-ton truck. You're still in the same weight class

to keep from compacting the ground, but you've got four more horsepower, power steering, and a live PTO and a water pump.

"It does sound like a good sleeper. I see them coming up all the time. Just a few years ago you could buy a nice, good-running one for $1,500 or $1,600. Do nothing but load it and take it to your house. And most of the time the late styled B was $800 more.

"The 50 did have some trouble with the PTO clutch on the live shaft. So did the 60. I think it was something that people weren't used to. The B and everything else was all one gearbox; you didn't take care of nothing. This required a little more maintenance and a little more experience."

— Frank Baker, Clarkrange, Tennessee

Model 520

Deere replaced the first Numbered series, as it's now known, with the 20 series for the 1956 to 1958 production years. The 520 replaced the 50, and like its predecessor, was only offered in one configuration: as a row-crop tractor. It was the smallest tractor on the Waterloo assembly line. In the gasoline and all-fuel versions it shipped at 4,960 pounds, compared to 5,858 pounds for the Model 620 and 7,800 pounds for the Model 720 coming off nearby assembly lines at the same time.

More important, for collectors, production also was lower. Deere built fewer than 14,000 units of the 520, making it the least popular of the 20 series row-crop tractors. For comparison, during the same period, Waterloo built approximately 23,000 of the midsize 620 and more than 31,000 of the larger 720. The smallest row-crop, the 420 series from Dubuque, was the most popular. Dubuque built more than 47,000 of these tractors.

In 1958, the 20 series era was closed and replaced by the 30 series models.

For today's collectors, the 520 is an excellent and sought-after midsize two-cylinder tractor. Market value is substantially more than the Model B or Model 50 for tractors in similar condition. The auction average sales value in 2004 and 2005 for 23 Model 520 tractors was about $3,800, within a narrow range of $500 to $6,000. The very best auction prices for a 520 have been running at about $2,000 more than for a 50.

A Model 520 LP row-crop tractor in original condition is ready for restoration work. Note the long rear axle. *Bruce Keller*

Models 520 and 50 had the same 190-ci engine. For size they were in the tradition of the Model B, but that's where the similarity ended. The 520 was a greatly improved and quite different tractor.

Drawbar power soared for the little gas engine, from only 16 horsepower in the Model B to 27 horsepower in the Model 50 to 33 horsepower on the Model 520. It had a better combustion chamber design, higher compression ratio, and a boost in rpm. The new engine speed was 1,325 rpm. The final drives were beefed up to handle the increased power, as was the transmission. Buyers had options for either an all-fuel or LP gas engine. The LP gas engine was nearly 300

A Model 520W is ready for restoration. This 1958 model in Missouri has a wide Norton front end and burns gas. *Dixon Somerville*

pounds heavier. The all-fuel engine, burning lower-octane fuel, produced slightly less power. Either of these is more collectable due to low production numbers. There were just 83 all-fuel versions and about 750 LP gas units entered in shipping records.

What the 520 lacked in variations, it made up for in options for front-end equipment. The standard front end was a dual-wheel tricycle. Options included Roll-O-Matic, a single wheel, an adjustable wide axle (48 to 80 inches wide), and a 38-inch fixed-tread axle.

The 1958 model had a few changes. An axle-mounted step became standard equipment. It had a black dash, sealed-beam lights, and a steering wheel with a plastic covering.

Collector demand for the 520 has been good over the past decade. The trend in value at auction has risen from about $2,700 in 1996 to about $3,700 at the end of 2005. Statistically, that's a 37 percent increase in value over 10 years, and for some it is a reasonable return on an investment. It's certainly a better return than the Model 50, though not as much as the Model B or 530.

Model 520 Buyers' Guide

"Resale on them are pretty high—50 series. They're a glorified B. An average 520 in fair working condition, I guess, will bring anywhere from $3,500 to $5,000."

— Don Doeden, Cook, Nebraska

"Just about all the 520s and 530s, even the 50s, check the manifold to make sure they're not cracked at all. Just about always that's going to be your first project.

"The late 520s and all the 530s had an oval muffler. If you've never been around them, you're used to buying a muffler for $40—you're getting ready to fall for $135 now. Your slanted dash steering wheel that you're paying $60 for just went to $135. But the battery box, seat cushions, and lights all interchange. The rest of the stuff, outside the sheet metal, the grilles, and all are the same."

— Frank Baker, Clarkrange, Tennessee

Model 530

Market demand makes the Model 530 one of the most highly valued John Deere two-cylinder tractors today. As an indicator,

This is a view of a 1958 Model 530 row-crop tractor with adjustable front axle.
John Dietz

the average sale value of a 530 at auction in 2005 was about $7,000, compared to $3,800 for the 520, $2,300 for the Model 50, and $1,900 for the Model B. The oldest members of the family of GP tractors were selling in the $5,000 range at the same time. As an investment over the 10-year period, the 530 was up at least 40 percent in value, according to the auction sales recorded in Machinery Pete.

Value, in this case, has more to do with position than factors like availability or unique characteristics. As a tractor, the Model 530 was nearly identical to the late Model 520 with a black dash. It had the same engine and drivetrain as the 520. In fact, most of the components are interchangeable. Sheet metal is the primary difference and the associated change in painting scheme.

Positionally, the 530 was among the last of the two-cylinder tractors, as was the entire 30 series. Collectors have shown a special affinity for that group. The entire 30 series

offers creature comforts with appeal today, such as power steering, electric start, lights, and excellent hydraulics. They make a comfortable ride for collectors old enough to remember driving Dad's new 530 nearly 50 years ago. In the case of the 530, it's also the smallest of the Waterloo-built 30 series tractors.

Model 530 was a GP row-crop tractor. The dual-tricycle front end was standard. Other front-end options included the dual-tricycle with Roll-O-Matic in regular or heavy-duty versions, a regular or heavy-duty single front wheel, an adjustable wide front axle, and a 38-inch, fixed-tread front axle.

Production of the 530 was lowest in the 30 series of row-crop tractors at approximately 10,300 tractors. Among the 530 series, production of all-fuel and LP gas models was much lower than the gasoline models, making them particularly collectable. Indications are that fewer than 100 of the all-fuel units were built.

The operator's view from the cockpit of a Model 530. *John Dietz*

This is the operator's chair and right-side controls on a Model 530. *John Dietz*

Model 530 Buyers' Guide

"The 530s are really getting to be pricey. The 520s are not that pricey, but they have gone up. A nice, real slick-fendered 520 will be $5,000, and with a wide front end it'll bring $6,500, but a 530 will bring anywhere from $8,500 to $10,000 or even $11,000.

"The brake shoes or brake pedals will interchange and work, but they don't look the same. On the 20 series, the place where you put your foot is not real wide, but on the 30 series, it's wide. A lot of guys rode with their foot on it and made the pedal go sideways. It really got real sloppy, and when it finally wore out, they could find a 20 series and throw that on. You'll see some come to a sale with one of each.

"Comparing the Bs to the 520s and 530s, that's the big seller—the power steering. It's not the three-point hitch. It's the power steering and the electric start.

"A lot of guys are telling me, now that they've had heart bypass surgery, that you lose a lot of that strength in your chest and your arms. Those guys are getting away from the row-crops and the bigger tractors, anything that doesn't have power steering, because they don't have the strength to handle it once they have their bypass."

— Frank Baker, Clarkrange, Tennessee

Start-Up Procedure for a Fence-Row Tractor

"In a nutshell, this is the procedure to start a tractor that's basically unknown. It would apply to just about any tractor. If the tractor turns over and you just want to get it running, there are a few basic steps. You won't be spending thousands of dollars, and you could end up with a very nice running tractor.

"If the engine is loose, do not even try to turn it over without making sure the valves are not stuck. You've got so much pressure in there that you could break the camshaft if you have a stuck valve.

"If it turns over but doesn't have compression, there are two likely problems. The valves may be crusted with rust or corrosion so they're not sealing, and they're allowing air to escape past them. Or the rings may be stuck in the groove, so air is going right past the rings and around the pistons.

"If we do have compression, we're not ready to start the tractor. The next major items are to rebuild the carburetor and to make sure the magneto is producing an adequate spark.

"Suppose this thing has been sitting for 30 years. A tremendous amount of condensation has accumulated in the crankcase and in the transmission. You must drain the engine, drain the transmission, drain the final drive housing, and then put in fresh lubrication.

"Old transmission grease and engine oil get really nasty. Dump at least a gallon of diesel fuel in the crankcase. Dump a gallon or maybe two gallons into the transmission. Hook it to another vehicle and just tow it around the yard for 15 or 20 minutes. The diesel fuel will act as a solvent and loosen and thin that old, heavy, hard grease. Then when you drain it, you've got a good possibility of washing out a lot of the debris. After that, put in your fresh lubricants.

"Now, I would attempt to start the engine. First check the oil pressure. If you don't have oil pressure, shut it down immediately and figure out why. On the GP, the oil pump is higher than the oil level in the crankcase. Over many years, oil will completely drain out and actually seal the oil pump. Sometimes you merely squirt some oil or 90-weight transmission lube into the relief valve port on the oil pump, turn it over, and suddenly you've got oil pressure.

"Once you have oil pressure, go ahead and start the engine.

"Since you don't know anything about the engine, listen to it very carefully. If there's a lot of clunking and banging, you've probably got a loose connecting rod or a wrist pin and it's time to shut her down right away. Then go after that problem."

—Cork Groth, Tractor Trauma Center, Eldridge, Iowa

Production and Ratings

Model	Variant	Fuel	Model Years	Number Produced	Stars
C	Kerosene	"	1928	180	*****
GP	Early, Small Bore	"	1928–1930	23,423	*
	Early, Big Bore	"	1928–1930	Unknown	
	Late, Big Bore	"	1930–1935	6,851	*
	Late, Oil Bath	"	1930–1935	Unknown	
	Tricycle	"	1928–1929	72	*****
	Orchard	"	1930–1935	717	***
GPWT	Small Bore	"	1929–1931	2,040	**
	Big Bore, Side Steer	"	1929–1931	769	***
	Overhead Steer	"	1932–1933	417	****
	Potato	"	1930	150	****
	Potato "from GP"	"	1930	73	*****
B	Short Frame	All-Fuel	1934–1936	40,057	*
	Long Frame	"	1937–1938	15,613	*
BN	Short Frame	"	1934–1936	807	***
	Long Frame	"	1937–1938	194	****
BW	Short Frame	"	1935–1936	207	****
	Long Frame	"	1937–1938	40	*****
BW-40	"	"	1936	6	*****
BNH	Long Frame	"	1937–1938	65	*****
BWH	"	"	1938	51	*****
BWH-40	"	"	1938	26 (est.)	*****
BR	Small Engine	"	1936–1938	6,404	*
BR	Big Engine	"	1939–1947	8,515	*
BR	Crawler	"	1939–1947	29	*****
BI	Crawler	"	1939–1947	1	*****
BO	Small Engine	"	1937–1938	5,083	*
	Big Engine	"	1939–1947	8,415	*
B	Early Styled	"	1939–1947	131,096	*
BN	Early Styled	"	1939–1947	3,584	**
BNH	Early Styled	"	1939–1947	446	****
BW	Early Styled	"	1939–1947	1,506	**
BWH	Early Styled	"	1939–1947	259	***
BWH-40	Early Styled	"	1939–1941	12	*****
B	Late Styled	Gas	1947–1952	89,334	*
B	Late Styled	All-Fuel	1947–1952	11,586	*
BN	Late Styled	Gas	1947–1952	3,913	**
BN	Late Styled	All-Fuel	1947–1952	608	***
BW	Late Styled	Gas	1947–1952	3,022	**
BW	Late Styled	All-Fuel	1947–1952	790	***
50	Gas	"	1953–1956	29,746	*
50	All-Fuel	"	1953–1956	2,097	**
50	LP	"	1955–1956	731	***
520	Gas	"	1956–1958	13,044	*
	All-Fuel	"	1956–1958	83	*****
	LP	"	1956–1958	764	***
530	Gas	"	1958–1960	9,813	*
	All-Fuel	"	1958–1960	85	*****
	LP	"	1958–1960	417	****

Specifications

Model	C/GP	B	50	520/530
Base price (1st year)	$850	$682	$2,100	$2,300/ $2,400
Width (in)	60	85	86.62	86.62
Height to radiator (in)	55.5	56	59.87	83.37
Length (in)	112	120.5	132.75	132.75
Weight (lb)	3,600	2,763	4,435	4,960
Front tires/wheels (in)	24x6	22x3.25	5.5x16	5.5x16
Rear tires/wheels (in)	42.75x10	48x5.25	10-38	12.4-36
Fuel capacity (gal)	16	13.5	15.5	18
Coolant capacity (qt)	9	6	7	4.5
Gears forward/reverse	3/1	4/1	6/1	6/1

Engine / Power Data

	Early A	Early AR	Styled A	Late A	Late AR
Fuel	Gas	All-fuel	All-fuel	Gas	Gas
Nebraska Test No.	222	378	335	384	429
Nebraska Test year	4/9/1934	10/27/1941	11/13/1939	6/7/1947	10/11/1949
Rated rpm	1,150	975	975	975	975
Bore and stroke (in)	4.25x5.25	5.5x6.75	5.5x6.75	5.6x6.75	5.6x6.75
Belt/PTO horsepower	16.01	30.33	29.59	38.02	39.1
Drawbar horsepower	11.84	26.52	26.2	34.14	34.9
Maximum pull	1,728	4,248	4,110	4,045	4,431
Shipping weight (lb)	3,275	6,350	6,410	6,574	7,367

Parts Prices

Model	GP Low	GP High	B Low	B High	50 Low	50 High	520 Low	520 High	530 Low	530 High
Air cleaner assembly							330		384	
Air cleaner intake stack			62	103			35		35	
Amp gauge			25	70	20	50	20	28	20	50
Battery box/cover			89	195	90	120	90	120	90	120
Battery cable (set)			26	38						
Block	300		200							
Camshaft			75	133			135			
Carburetor	400	474	260	543	260	543	260	500	500	
Carburetor float	23		23	36	25	28	25	28	25	28
Carburetor kit	17	30	20	30	20	45	20	45	20	45
Clutch drive disc										
Clutch pulley cover			30	50	33	35	33	35	33	35
Clutch slider disc										
Connecting rod	60		55	194	210	255	115	125	115	
Crankshaft	180									
Cylinder head	280		315	436			351	392		
Dash										
Distributor					190	283	190	205	170	205
Distributor cap			30	55	15	30	17		17	

Model	GP Low	High	B Low	High	50 Low	High	520 Low	High	530 Low	High
Drag links	70									
Engine overhaul kit			294	333						
Exhaust manifold										
Exhaust pipe			21	136	24	110	24	110	24	110
Fan assembly										
Fender			137	217	129	164	150	200	150	200
Flywheel	150		75	125						
Flywheel cover			25	150						
Fuel tank										
Generator			120	179	125	179	125	179	125	179
Grille screen			15	60	35	45	35	45	35	45
Grille with screen			290							
Headlight assembly			37	75	37	67	49	75	57	75
Magneto	265	365	249	375	310					
Manifold (intake & exhaust)	150		100	245	160	220	156	245	156	245
Muffler			20	90	20	90	18	90	18	90
Overhaul kit (piston, rings, etc.)			275	650	275	458	275	579	275	579
Pan seat	85		35	55						
Piston										
Piston rings			69	119	99	129	99	129	99	129
PTO shield			60	75	60	112	75	146	75	146
Radiator	300		155	230	230		230		230	
Radiator cap	55	78	19	90	13	25	6	15	6	25
Radiator core	205	265	133	249	116	230	116	230	116	230
Seat cushion (bottom)			28	50	28	60	28	60	28	60
Sediment bowl			45							
Spark plug wires (set)	13	17	13	16	11	13	13		11	13
Starter			125	162	125	249	260		260	
Starter drive assembly			19	30			45		45	
Steering wheel			44	70	44	65	44	140	44	140
Three-point hitch			410	693	410	693	325	647	325	647
Toolbox			30	50						
Voltage regulator			37		37	52	37	52	37	52
Water pump			105	181	105	181	97	181	105	181
Weight, front					167		167		167	
Wheel bearings			39	73	39	73	39		39	
Wheel weights (405-lb set)					375		375		375	

Ratings
Collector's 5-Star Editions

Model	Fuel	
BWH	All-Fuel	51
BW Long Frame	All-Fuel	40
BR Crawler	All-Fuel	29
BWH-40	All-Fuel	26 (est.)
BWH-40 Styled	All-Fuel	12
BW-40	All-Fuel	6
BR Crawler	All-Fuel	1
C	All-Fuel	180

Average Sale Value 1995 to 2010 (Actual and Projected)

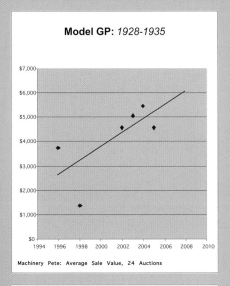

Model GP: *1928-1935*

Machinery Pete: Average Sale Value, 24 Auctions

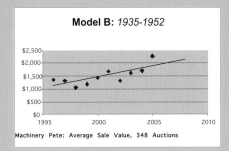

Model B: *1935-1952*

Machinery Pete: Average Sale Value, 348 Auctions

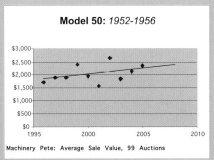

Model 50: *1952-1956*

Machinery Pete: Average Sale Value, 99 Auctions

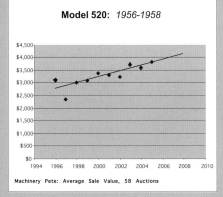

Model 520: *1956-1958*

Machinery Pete: Average Sale Value, 58 Auctions

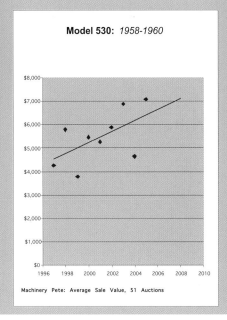

Model 530: *1958-1960*

Machinery Pete: Average Sale Value, 51 Auctions

This is a Model 730 Hi-Crop diesel that was repatriated from Argentina. *Bruce Keller*

Chapter 5

Models G, 70, 720, 730

The Model G and its successors, the 70, 720, and 730, were the largest row-crop tractors in Deere's two-cylinder era. They were built on Waterloo assembly lines between 1937 and 1960. Total production reached about 163,000 tractors, which is less than half the midsize Model A and is even smaller than Model B production. Models A, B, and G went through the Nebraska Tractor Test in June 1938. The Model G was rated for three 14-inch plows and weighed 4,400 pounds. The Model A handled two 16-inch plows and weighed 3,783 pounds. The Model B was the lightweight at 2,878 pounds and was rated for two 14-inch plows. A lot of steel was added to these tractors over the next 20 years. For the final Nebraska test in 1958, within the 720 and 730 series, weights ranged from 6,790 pounds to 8,470 pounds for the hi-crop diesel version. These tractors need serious equipment for hauling and significant space for storage, plus some heavy shop equipment for anyone planning to work on one.

The Model G family is distinguished for collectors by the impact of World War II. Deere left this as the final row-crop family for styling. Along with the styled treatment, tractor price also had to increase. It turned out that the styled G was to be introduced in early 1942, less than three months after Pearl Harbor was bombed. The new War Production Board introduced a regulation that prohibited the planned price increase. Rather than leave the tractor as an unstyled ugly duckling, Deere changed the model name. In place of the Model G, Deere began building the modernized 1942 Model GM tractor.

A second wartime hit came six months later, in September 1942. Deere actually suspended production of the Model GM for the next 24 months. When production of this family resumed in October 1944, new tractors coming off the line were identified as the 1945 model. The 1944 GM never got off the drawing board. When GM production finally resumed, it was at a slower pace than the smaller and better-selling Model A and Model B tractors.

When the war ended, the GM name disappeared but nearly identical Model G tractors rolled off the assembly lines. For the first time some variation in model production was introduced. The Model G was replaced in the 1950s by the Model 70, then the 20 series, and finally the 30 series, which was true to Deere's general policy of changing model names from letter to number.

Many, or most, surviving tractors in this family have made their way into personal collections. By sheer size and weight, they are powerful tractors, as well as reliable. They are certainly available, though they are less common at rural auction sales. Parts are mostly available for restoration work. Value has been increasing with time and is more than a non-collector might expect. Two have doubled in value in the past 10 years. Value in relation to the Model A and Model B families also is somewhat higher, given the same age, configuration, and condition. The last of the Model G series, the 730, was the heaviest two-cylinder production tractor that Deere ever built and costs a bit more in the auction ring than the 530 or the 630.

Model G

Deere & Company postponed introduction of the Model G until the Great Depression released its grip. Deere had been developing its version of a row-crop tractor since the success of the Model D a decade earlier. Its first production unit, dubbed the Model C, was promoted as an all-crop row-crop tractor. The first two short production runs were built in 1927 and

Built on January 5, 1938, this is the low-radiator version of the Model G with factory decals and spoke wheels with extension wheels. *Eddie Campbell*

1928. With a new name and some changes, Deere's Model GP was on the assembly line on August 2, 1928. Field reports on GP performance arrived in 1929, providing grist for change. On October 24, 1929, also known as Black Thursday, the stock market crashed. Sales numbers plunged. Field reports on GP performance, unlike the faithful Model D, were grim. While the economy recovered, developers had time for reflection.

One result was a decision to build row-crop tractors in three distinct sizes for different markets. The first off the line was the Model A, in 1934, with 24 horsepower on the belt. It was followed almost immediately by the Model B, the smallest of the Waterloo row-crop tractors and direct successor to the GP. Initially, the Model B had just 18 horsepower. Both row-crop tractors came back with big sales and glowing field reports. Thus, in 1937, Deere launched the biggest and best row-crop tractor, the 36-horsepower Model G.

The new Model G had power to handle a wide variety of jobs, including four-row cultivators and planters. It also could drive a threshing machine at full capacity with steady, high-torque power generated by a totally new two-cylinder engine. This engine had a whopping 413-ci displacement. The four-speed transmission and final drives were appropriately

re-engineered to handle all the new power. Mechanically, the well-maintained Model G was likely to outlive its owner.

Wartime shortages had more impact on Model G production than on the two smaller row-crop families. It affected the supply then, and today their value is affected.

Soon after the Model G entered field service in spring 1937, owners had issues with the cooling system. Pulling heavy loads in a hot climate was easy enough for the big engine, but the cooling system tended to overheat. Deere solved the problem quickly and inadvertently created a subset for collectors to pursue. The early G now is known as the low-radiator G, as distinguished from the later high-radiator G. The latter went into production on January 19, 1938. The revised Model G has a larger, taller radiator along with a revised fan and shroud, revised radiator shutter, and a larger fuel tank. The hood and some other parts also are a little different. Identification is easy. The top of the taller radiator tank was redesigned, and a new groove provided clearance for the steering shaft. On the earlier low-radiator models, the steering shaft clears the top of the radiator by about a half inch.

Approximately 1,600 Model G tractors rolled off the assembly line in the first season. When the assembly line

This 1941 edition was the end of the unstyled G line. *Ron Jungmeyer*

The styled GM was built during World War II and replaced the unstyled Model G. *Bruce Keller*

This 1951 late styled G row-crop tractor has been restored to pristine condition and is ready for a showroom. The series was reintroduced and expanded in 1947 to include four configurations.
Ron Jungmeyer

began building new 1938 models a couple of months later, workers began setting the exhaust valves an eighth inch deeper in the cylinder head to improve heat transfer. In the field, dealerships offered a modification program. It reached most, but not all, of the 1,600 early low-radiator G tractors. Models in the cooler northern states and Canada had escaped the overheating issue and sometimes escaped the modification. Today, a few privileged collectors have the original, unmodified, low-radiator G to prove the story.

For the 1939 model year, the cylinder block and head were modified to provide more efficient heat transfer and coolant flow. In turn, a new upper water pipe was required.

Collectors should be cautious. The Model G had quite a few other changes before the last 600-plus 1942 models rolled off the assembly line on December 22, 1941. Parts may or may not be interchangeable. Appropriate parts books are available from Deere Service Publications (1-800-522-7448).

In total, less than 10,700 Model G tractors were built before 1942. They are not as easy to find as an A or B and are harder to haul around. They need a bigger garage or shed, but they are somewhat more collectable. Model G tractors are simple and easy to understand and operate. They have quite a variety of steel and rubber wheel options. Parts tend to be more expensive. At auction they tend to be pricey for good reason.

The low-radiator G is the highest valued in the family. One sold in 2004 for $13,500 and another in 2005 for $16,000, at the John Deere Collectors' Center annual sale. The value trend in the Model G family has increased from about $2,200 10 years ago to about $4,500 today, according to the tracking at www.machinerypete.com. It's also quite possible that a Model G purchased in 1996 at one auction for $2,000 could have sold for up to $6,000 in 2005, depending on factors like auction location, the nature of the auction, and who was there. This model would have been a good investment and probably still is.

Model GM

The styled and modernized Model GM was introduced in early 1942, while the Model G was suspended. Sales were slow, as had been the case with the Model G in comparison to the smaller row-crop tractors. Approximately 750 GM tractors were built in 1942 before production was suspended due to material shortages. It took about twice the steel and other metals to build a GM as opposed to the styled B. The

Detail view of the Model G engine compartment and nose. *Ron Jungmeyer*

1942 GMs represented two model years, 1942 and 1943, but none were built in 1943. Production resumed in October 1944 with the 1945 model on the assembly line. When the war ended, it wasn't long before Deere cancelled the GM series. Waterloo had built approximately 8,800 GM tractors. For collectors today, the GM isn't rare, but it certainly is harder to find than the basic Model A or Model B. And it has some interesting history.

If you could get one, the GM was an excellent and good-looking two-cylinder tractor for a large farm. It had an improved powertrain, as well as styled sheet metal. The engine ran cooler. Some internal engine changes gave it a bit more power. It had an improved Marvo Schivler DLTX 51 ("Big Nut") carburetor. A new six-speed transmission handled by a two-lever shift system was available, though it was in short supply. Shutter controls were improved. One thing that didn't change was the side-by-side air intake and exhaust stack arrangement (on the styled A and B, these had been switched to an inline arrangement).

Electric starting and lighting were optional on the big tractor. Other options included Power Lift and fenders. Product development and sales were at a near standstill for the

big row-crop tractor during the war years. In October 1945, with the war over, Deere introduced Powr-Trol as an option for all its row-crop tractors, including the GM. For the first time, the tractor could operate a remote hydraulic cylinder and do precision positioning of the rockshaft.

Restoration people who have wanted to replace a Model GM flywheel have one warning for collectors. In the GM design process, Deere modified the Model G flywheel so it would have clearance with the styled GM design, and they gave the new design a new part number. However, Deere failed to change the casting number, so there now are two slightly different flywheels with the same casting number.

Collectors sometimes specialize in steel wheels, trying to equip their tractors with the variations. Model GM could make a good project. They were built with four variations in steel wheels, but only two are likely to be found in North America. Historian J. R. Hobbs has written of this: "Steel wheels for the GM are hard to find and expensive, as are the rare hand crank flywheels. Only 962 GM tractors were shipped on steel and 342 of them were exported."[6] When these big tractors left Waterloo on steel wheels, they also left with only four forward

A 1950 styled Model G in Nebraska with the adjustable wide front axle. *Bill Becker*

gears. A six-gear transmission was available, but field speed at more than 6 miles per hour on steel was dangerous.

As a collector's item, the GM has a lot of potential. Only 16 GM auction sales reports are available for consideration over the past 10 years. Considering the number built, this model doesn't come up at auction very often. Auction value generally has been between $2,000 and $4,000. However, in 2005 two sold for $5,000 and one brought $11,000.

Styled G

Unlike the G and GM, collectors can find some diversity in the styled Model G family, built for model years 1947 through 1953. They can look for the early styled G or the late styled G, and subsets in each. There is a good supply of the late styled G, as production reached nearly 32,000 units. On the other hand, the early styled G was phased out after only five months of production and about 2,600 units. The early styled G had two versions, and the late styled G had three versions. Any of these small subsets are highly collectable.

The first styled G rolled off the assembly line on March 7, 1947. It looked about the same as the last few GMs that were still being assembled, but it had only a G on the serial number plate, rather than GM. This styled G also had the Roll-O-Matic knee action option, a choice already popular on the smaller row-crop tractors. It had electric lighting and a starter, but those farmers who preferred the old and reliable hand crank for starting and steel wheels in the field still could order it for their styled G.

A Model 70 tractor with adjustable wide front axle. These tractors replaced the Model G. *John Dietz*

With veterans now at home and farms modernizing, Deere executives decided it was time to offer row-crop farmers some configuration options on the biggest row-crop tractor. The split pedestal, already used on Model A and B tractors, was retooled for the larger G family. The factory began taking orders for narrow, single front-wheel GN versions and wide-axle GW versions. The GW could be ordered with adjustable rear axles to make the configuration as versatile as growers' needs. With the 104-inch rear axle, the biggest row-crop tractor now was well suited for narrow row-crops and for crops grown on raised beds.

The late styled G, introduced at the end of July 1947 as a 1947 model, was a bit more comfortable. It had a box-style seat instead of the old pan seat. Batteries were under the seat in a more convenient location. It had a few cosmetic changes, along with a belt pulley guard to prevent dirt and oil from flying into the operator's face.

After this, the late styled G, GN, and GW tractors saw quite a number of minor changes. It's never safe to assume the parts are interchangeable. The camshaft and bearings changed, the PTO shaft was standardized, there was a new distributor, a new water pump, and a steel radiator core. There were numerous wheel options. The G, GN, and GW had six options for rear wheels on steel or rubber, and there were several versions for front wheels.

Finally, for 1951, Deere responded to sugarcane growers in Louisiana and Florida with a hi-crop Model G. The 412-ci GH all-fuel engine was less expensive to operate than the late

This Model 70 standard LP version was built in 1955 and has been beautifully restored. The sheet metal was all green until the 20 series was introduced about a year later. *John Detmer*

styled A and provided a heavier machine for the work. At 154 inches, it was the longest production tractor in the two-cylinder family and was the tallest tractor to that point in time. Over two model years, Waterloo built about 240 GH tractors and exported half. The few survivors are very valuable. One G Hi-Crop, fully restored and with new tires, sold at a Minnesota auction in 2003 for $32,000, and another sold for $27,000.

What Deere didn't do with the G is interesting. Deere never built a standard tread GR tractor, similar to the AR or BR. Deere also never supplied an LP gas, diesel, or gasoline version of the G, although some options were provided by aftermarket suppliers.

Styled Gs aren't particularly differentiated in the sales reports, but it appears that buyers will pay more for the newer, postwar styled G family than for Gs that preceded the GM.

Model G Buyers' Guide

"I tell all our clients that if you're going to buy just one or two [tractors], get into the Gs or something like that, but don't buy an A or B because everybody's got one of those. If you're going to take it to show, have something to show. If you're into it for investment plus the ability to say I've got John Deere tractors, go with the rare stuff first. You can always find the common stuff later.

"If you're going to a consignment sale to buy a tractor, be leery. You want to know what you're looking for. Sometimes it's cheaper than it would be at an estate sale, but not always. Your estate auctions will be 20 percent higher than market value, most times. Consignment sales will run about average to 10 percent low. If I was going to look for a tractor to buy for myself, the private sale is the way to go rather than consignment."

— Glen Parker, Deeres of Yesteryear, Poseyville, Indiana

"I've been in the business here for 7½ years. I have customers from most of the United States, Australia, England, Denmark. We've sent a trailer-load of stuff to Denmark. It seems like tractors are getting harder to come up with because people are collecting them and just holding onto anything they can get a hold on. There's a lot of stuff that's no longer available.

"Unstyled G parts are hard to find. The DLTX 51 Big Nut G carburetors are getting scarce. The 70 parts are out there, but not many. There's very few new parts out there for a 70. Seems like the gears and everything for a 70 just about have to be used. I can still get a lot of used parts on the 720 and 730."

— Kevin Hill, Two-Cylinder Plus Tractor Salvage, Conway, Missouri

This restored Model 70 diesel makes a fantastic lawn ornament in Florida. Note the teardrop-shaped flywheel cover for the diesel version. *Frank Boerger*

Another postcard from the Ohio woods! This is a 1955 Model 70 standard diesel. *Dave Hadam*

Model 70

A good question to ask when someone starts talking about a John Deere 70 is "Which one?" This successor to the late styled G was only built from 1953 through 1956, but it was available in three configurations and with four types of fuel. Throw in the model year, and you've got 32 possible answers to the question without going into any more detail. During the previous 16 years, Deere had built approximately 60,000 units in its largest row-crop tractor family. Most years, sales had been slow. The best sales had been 32,000 of the late styled G tractors in six years. Now, in just four years, Deere built and sold more than 41,000 Model 70 tractors.

This is a 1958 Model 720 row-crop diesel with a pony engine start that was lovingly restored for a personal collection in Missouri. *Eddie Campbell*

The Model 70 also was a very different tractor from the Model G. It had an all-new engine, improved operator features and comfort, better hydraulics, live PTO, power steering, rack-and-pinion rear tread adjustment, and a 12-volt electrical system. It continued using the same high-low transmission as the Model G and now weighed about 6,000 pounds.

Deere had switched to a basic number designation for new models of two-cylinder tractors by the time it was ready to revise the late styled Model G. The new Model A had been designated as the Model 60 in June 1952. Late in the year, the Model 50 replaced the Model B. Now, in April 1953, Deere unveiled its latest, biggest, and best row-crop tractor, the Model 70 with a choice of gasoline or all-fuel engine.

The 70 was a very different tractor from its predecessor. It had more power, more weight, and more comfort than ever before. Like the others in this first Numbered series, it remains largely bypassed by collectors who favor the unstyled early tractors or one of the last in the 30 series, built between 1958 and 1960. However, in its day, the 70 was a very popular tractor, and a new time for it may come again.

The basic row-crop Model 70 had the same all-fuel engine as the G family. It had developed into a very good engine.

A rural Manitoba restoration project is ready to be torn down. This is another Model 720 standard version in original condition. *John Dietz*

In the Model 70, thanks to a new dual-barrel carburetor and improved distributor, it produced 6 more horsepower with almost no backfire issues.

Here's the end product from a great restoration: a 1957 Model 720 standard LP tractor. *John Detmer*

The big Model 720 was well equipped for loader work. This one has the Number 50 self-leveling loader. *Eddie Campbell*

Deere developed a gasoline engine for the Model 70. It was smaller than the all-fuel engine at 379 cubic inches, but it had more power. It had the same duplex carburetor, somewhat higher compression, and an improved cylinder-head design.

A year later, Deere began offering a third engine option: LP gas. The LP system was factory engineered and not an add-on. It achieved nearly 52 horsepower on the Nebraska test, which is the highest of the Model 70 engine series.

A split front pedestal now was standard, enabling Deere to offer five front-end choices for configuration: standard dual front wheels, Roll-O-Matic front wheels, a single front wheel, a 38-inch fixed tread front axle, and a width-adjustable front axle. At the rear, there were options for long or extra-long axles with tread from 56 to 112 inches.

The Model 70 came equipped with Powr-Trol for live hydraulic power and had an option for a live PTO. It had a

One of the last existing tractors of its kind, this 1960 Model 730 row-crop diesel version with electric start is too pretty to work again. *Eddie Campbell*

new 800 series three-point hitch. Factory-engineered power steering became available in 1954 and came with a smaller three-spoke steering wheel.

Another configuration, the 70S with standard tread front and rear, was available for the 1954 models. Only three were built that year: two with the gasoline engine and one with LP gas. However, standard tread sales took off and more than 3,000 were built over the following two model years.

The fourth fuel option, diesel, was available for 1955 and 1956 models in either the row-crop, standard tread, or hi-crop configuration. The diesel version was very popular and led to sales of 14,397 tractors in just two years, even though it added about 25 percent to the purchase price.

The Model 70 was Deere's first row-crop tractor that burned diesel. It was more economical to operate than the big diesel-burning Model R that had just ended its seven-year production run. In fact, the Model 70 diesel broke the all-time fuel-economy record at Nebraska that had been held by the John Deere Model R. The Model 70 diesel turned out 51.5 horsepower on the belt and 54.7 horsepower on the drawbar. A new center main bearing for the crankshaft helped keep the crankshaft in place while it was under load and provided better balance for the engine.

Owners started this 376-ci, high-compression diesel with the aid of the new V-4 gasoline-fired starting engine. The little four-cylinder gas engine provided unlimited cranking time for the diesel. Its exhaust warmed the diesel's intake air. The two engines shared one cooling system. The pony engine was started by pushing a lever forward. When the V-4 was running steady, the operator pulled the lever back to engage the flywheel ring gear and turn the big diesel engine. When the diesel was turning over, the lever was moved partially forward to put the diesel on full compression and operate alone.

The 1956 Model 70 saw several minor changes. Probably the most popular was the new 801 Traction-Trol hitch. It provided a mechanical weight transfer to the rear wheels from implements mounted on the hitch to give more traction. Many of the earlier 800 and 800A hitches were replaced with the 801, which now is a collector's item worth several hundred dollars.

Diesel engines in the Model 70, 720, and 730 had a common problem that should be noted. Over time, the flywheel became loose on the crankshaft. The flywheel was built with softer metal than the crank and both were splined with only one key. Eventually, the weight of the flywheel rocking to a stop against the splines became too much and led to a loose flywheel. Operators could prevent the problem by shutting off the diesel and releasing compression with

This is a 1959 Model 730 row-crop diesel version with a wide front. *John Detmer*

This 1959 Model 730 row-crop LP version is part of a Canadian collection. *Elmer Friesen*

A 1959 Model 730 row-crop has a gasoline engine and an umbrella for the heat. It looks like this one gets to see some work yet.
Eddie Campbell

A low-production late 1958 edition of the Model 730 standard gas version.
John Dietz

the decompression lever. This eliminated nearly all of the rocking action.

The 70 series has both rare and common tractors for collectors. The biggest run was more than 6,200 row-crop diesel units in 1955. On the other hand, the 70 Hi-Crop is rare. As reported by *Green Magazine*, Waterloo only built 157 of these, with production ranging from 16 to 69 tractors, depending on the type of fuel, or 8 to 63 tractors, depending on the year. Current values reflect the supply. In this family, the highest recorded auction sale value through 2005 was for a 70 Hi-Crop that burned diesel fuel. Only 44 of these were built in the two model years, and this one sold for $33,000 at the 2001 Collectors Center sale.

While values for rare members of the Model 70 family have been rising sharply, the general specimen has done well but remained a low-cost item in the market. Like other Number series tractors, the 70 is less eagerly pursued at this point by collectors than the later 20 and 30 series tractors in the family. In 1996, a good-running Model 70 row-crop could be purchased for $2,000 or less. Ten years later, the value of that unit has increased at least 60 percent. A 70 that looks and sounds good, without anything special, may go for more than $4,000 at auction. For the Waterloo-built Numbered series tractors, the 70 in today's market still has a nice premium over the 50 or 60, and is only now at about the market value that the big 80 was 10 years ago.

Model 70 Buyers' Guide

"There's a lot of things to watch out for. You see it all at these consignment sales, because they doctor it up to get it through the line. The 70 diesels had particularly bad crankshafts, and it's in the early 720s, too. The green dash 720 had problems with the crankshaft. Governors are another thing [to watch] on all the tractors. The governor will run, but it doesn't run well. When you tear into it, you get into the clutch."

— Glen Parker, Deeres of Yesteryear, Poseyville, Indiana

Model 720

The John Deere Model 720 became, and remains, a very popular tractor. It has doubled in value in the antique tractor market over the past decade. It was a direct replacement for the already popular Model 70. It was promoted as a five-plow tractor and

That's a sharp-looking slanted black dash and instrument cluster on the 730. If a gauge needs to be replaced, it can easily be done in your garage. *John Dietz*

was able to replace two tractors on many farms for plowing and disking. It handled as easily as most small tractors.

During a short three-year run, Deere built 30,675 tractors in the Model 720 series. The series continued giving growers options for gasoline, all-fuel, LP gas, or diesel fuel engines. It was available in four configurations: row-crop dual-wheel, row-crop wide front, standard tread, and hi-crop. The engines had major improvements, such as a new alloy steel crankshaft, heavier connecting rods, larger piston pins, improved cyclonic swirl in the combustion chamber, and higher rpm.

The business end of a 730 is 1950s technology at its best. It was heavy duty and very reliable. *John Dietz*

It may look small on this big tractor, but the little V-4 starter engine that isn't working right can hurt as bad as a tooth-ache. It can be repaired, but it's very expensive for its size. *John Dietz*

The 720 was the largest two-cylinder, row-crop tractor built by Deere and tested at Nebraska. The high-crop version was the tallest of the two-cylinder tractors and measured 8 feet, 5 inches tall, and was nearly the longest tractor at 12 feet, 4³⁄₁₆ inches. The 720 set numerous records, such as 56.84 belt horsepower with gasoline and set a new fuel economy record. Engine displacement was a little less, but Deere set its operating speed at 1,125 rpm. Previous engines in the Model G and Model 70 tractors had turned at 975 rpm. As well, Deere improved the pistons, cylinder head, and ignition system.

This also was a heavier tractor that hit the scale at 6,800 pounds in the row-crop version—about 660 pounds heavier than its big and beefy Model 70 predecessor, and at 8,470 pounds in the diesel high-crop version. A 1,000-rpm PTO was optional, although it seldom was ordered. The Model 720 had a six-speed transmission that replaced the outdated high-low-range Model G transmission that had continued into the Model 70, and it had a much improved three-point hitch.

The popular diesel engine version kept the same specs as the Model 70 diesel for engine bore and stroke. The diesel version came with the V-4 pony engine that now used two levers rather than one. One lever decompressed the engine and the other engaged the pony pinion to the flywheel ring gear. A 24-volt electric starting system was added as an option in February 1958. Late in the run, the big diesel engine got a new antireverse camshaft with better lobe profiles. It prevented the possibility that the diesel engine could start to run backward when it was being shut down.

The four engines went through the Nebraska tests around the same time. In round numbers, the LP gas recorded 52 drawbar and 57 belt horsepower. The gasoline engine recorded 53 drawbar and 57 belt horsepower. The diesel recorded 51 drawbar and 56 belt horsepower. The tractor fuel (all-fuel) version recorded the lowest results, 40 drawbar and 44 belt horsepower.

This was a comfortable place to work most of the time. Notable features were the power steering and Float-Ride seat. *John Dietz*

The basic Model 720 with its split pedestal was by far the most popular version. Nearly 23,000 copies were built. Deere built 4,500 of the Model 720 standard tractors. Nearly 3,600 of these tractors were diesel. Only 80 had the all-fuel option, and most of those were exported. The 720S could be ordered with either a 55.5-inch fixed-tread front axle or an adjustable axle with 52- to 58-inch tread.

Any Model 720 that's been maintained is worth more today than 10 years ago, and a 720 Hi-Crop is worth a lot more. Average auction sale value in 2005 in the 720 family

was at $5,000 or more, as compared to about $2,500 in 1996. Machinery Pete auctioneers reported 22 sales of Model 720 tractors just in 2005. None sold for less than $3,600 and none for more than $7,500. Had a special one been offered, it would have gone for more. For instance, a fully restored diesel 720 Hi-Crop with pony start came up for sale in 2003 at the Deere Collectors Center auction. It sold for $55,000. Apparently Deere only built a total of about 160 of the 730 Hi-Crop tractors. The set subdivides into four different fuel types. If only three were built and you can get one, it's very unlikely that your neighbor will ever get one of the other two!

Model 730

The John Deere Model 730 two-cylinder tractor is another excellent commodity in the antique-tractor market if you're into big tractors. It was truly the last of the two-cylinder tractors. It had all the bells and whistles of two-cylinder craftsmanship. It was one step down from the largest power unit, the 9,875-pound diesel 830, but it was designed for row-crop work and was more versatile on the farm. Where the 830 had one purpose, to perform the heaviest drawbar and belt work on expansive fields of grain, the 730 could do nearly all of that while providing the steering accuracy and power assistance required for row-crops. It was a thoroughly modern, highly capable tractor. After more than 45 years of service, many are still at work and are far too precious to be considered as collectable antiques.

The 30 series was introduced in 1958, just two years after the major upgrades that had gone into developing the 20 series. By 1958, Deere was well along in gearing up for its New Generation tractors with four cylinders. The first of these, the mighty 8010, was introduced in September 1959. Thus, the 30 series was the terminal line of Deere's two-cylinder tractors and Deere chose not to invest in major alterations for the 30 series. The focus for marketing was operator comfort and more modern styling. It worked. Ever since this whole series of tractors has been dear to owners and collectors.

Styling changes were common to the 30 series. At a distance, the painting scheme was quite different. Up close, these tractors came with a new sloping, automobile-style steering wheel and a sloping dash where instruments were

The hood on a 30 series tractor can be replaced if necessary. Waterloo shortened the 20 series hood as part of the development process for the 30 series, and it's been done since then in restoration shops. *John Dietz*

Matching levers decompress and engage the pup engine for starting the big 730 diesel. The foot-operated left brake pedal can be seen below. *John Dietz*

clustered for easy viewing by the driver. As well, the 30 series row-crop tractors came with headlights. It was an important styling innovation, as well as highly practical.

The Model 730 was Deere's biggest row-crop tractor and a mechanical twin to the 720. Variations to the row-crop included the standard and hi-crop. All three were available with a six-speed transmission and four engine choices: gasoline, all-fuel, LP gas, or diesel. Rubber tires were standard, although it was still possible to order steel front or rear wheels. Basics on the Model 730 included power steering, an adjustable front axle, three-point hitch, Float-Ride seat, precleaner and air stack, dish-type rear wheel, and dual hydraulics. The 730 diesel had options for the V-4 starting engine or a 24-volt electric starter. The 730 had styled flattop rear fenders with an improved lighting system for work at night. For operator safety, the fenders had handholds that protected the operator from mud, dust, and possible contact with the tires. A convenient step in front of the rear axle made mounting and dismounting both safer and easier.

At Waterloo, the Model 730 was the end of the line for two-cylinder tractors. The two-cylinder assembly lines in

Model 730 Buyers' Guide

"I haven't run into sheet metal that isn't available on these 20 and 30 series tractors other than on a 620 propane tractor. That stuff is fairly hard to find. We were able to take a hood from a regular standard tractor and cut it so that it fit. That's what they did to begin with; they shortened the hoods up. You can do those kinds of things."

— Harvey Hamilton, Tired Iron Restoration, Oakville, Washington

"Another thing that's in short supply and a typical problem on these old tractors, especially with the bigger ones, is the crankshaft and flywheel. A lot of times the flywheel will get loose and the pounding of the two-cylinder engine will make that big heavy flywheel rock back and forth. It destroys the splines on the crankshaft and makes the flywheel unusable, too. I've tried to find used flywheels and haven't had any luck.

Model 730 standard diesel. *John Dietz*

"The little starting engines for diesels, are expensive little rascals to fix. We're talking about $1,500 in parts, just for the little crankshaft, some sleeves, and pistons. . . . If you can get a good little cranking engine with the tractor, that's money ahead." — Harvey Hamilton, Tired Iron Restoration, Oakville, Washington

"In 1994, you could buy that 30 LP standard for a couple thousand dollars. Today, they bring $20,000. It is a good investment. Some of our clientele use it for that. They take money out of CDs and buy tractors because of the increasing value." — Glen Parker, Deeres of Yesteryear, Poseyville, Indiana

Waterloo shut down for the last time on March 1, 1961, after more than 40 years of production. The 730 assembly line and production tooling were packed onto a boat and shipped to Deere's new facility in Rosario, Argentina. New Model 730 tractors started rolling off the Argentina assembly line and continued there until 1970. More than 20,000 Argentinean Model 730 tractors were built. Deere also assembled other Model 730s at a plant in Monterey, Mexico.

Before the 1961 shutdown, Waterloo built nearly 30,500 units of the 730 for the North American market. Nearly all were row-crop versions. About 3,200 were in the standard configuration and about 230 were hi-crop models.

Auction sales records indicate the value of a typical Model 730 has doubled over the past 10 years. Recorded sales of 26 units in 1996 clustered around $3,750, plus or minus $500. Two sold in the range of $6,000 to $7,000. Auction sales are recorded for 36 of these tractors in 2004 and 2005. They cluster now at about $6,000, give or take $1,000, but the exceptions are huge. Seven sold for $10,000 or more, pushing the average sale value in the two-year period to just over $8,000. Without the high value sales, the underlying increased value is about 60 percent compared to a decade ago.

The 730 standard, either LP gas or diesel, is a little more valuable than average. A repatriated Argentine 730 diesel sold for $16,000 in 2005. The hi-crop is a rare item. Two sales in 2005 are worthy of note. One sold in an Iowa auction for $46,000; the other, an LP gas version, sold for $82,500.

Production and Ratings

Model	Variant	Fuel	Model Years	Number Produced	Stars
G	Unstyled	All-Fuel	1937–1941	10,684	*
GM	"		1942–1947	8,764	**
G	Early Styled	"	1947	2,403	**
GN	Early Styled	"	1947	49	*****
GW	Early Styled	"	1947	120	****
G	Late Styled	"	1948–1953	31,913	*
GN	Late Styled	"	1948–1953	1,522	**
GW	Late Styled	"	1948–1953	4,666	**
GH	Late Styled	"	1952–1953	235	****
70	"	Gas	1953–1956	16,000	*
70	"	All-Fuel	1953–1956	2,509	**
70	"	LP	1954–1956	6,254	**
70	"	Diesel	1955–1956	11,105	*
70	R	Gas	1954–1956	1,035	**
70	R	All-Fuel	1955–1956	385	****
70	R	LP	1954–1956	336	****
70	R	Diesel	1955–1956	3,248	**
70	HC	Gas	1953–1956	16	*****
70	HC	All-Fuel	1954–1956	69	*****
70	HC	LP	1954–1956	28	*****
70	HC	Diesel	1955–1956	44	*****
720	"	Gas	1956–1958	19,950	*
	"	All-Fuel	1956–1958	408	****
	"	LP	1956–1958	3,670	**
	"	Diesel	1956–1958	3,000	**
720	S	Gas	1956–1958	520	***
	"	All-Fuel	1956–1958	80	*****
	"	LP	1956–1958	345	****
	"	Diesel	1956–1958	3,578	**
720	H	Gas	1956–1958	5	*****
	"	All-Fuel	1956–1958	12	*****
	"	LP	1956–1958	22	*****
	"	Diesel – Pony	1956–1958	77	*****
	"	Diesel – Elec	1956–1958	9	*****
730	"	Gas	1959–1960	3,560	**
	"	All-Fuel	1959–1960	177	****
	"	LP	1959–1960	3,263	**
	"	Diesel – Pony	1959–1960	3,703	**
	"	Diesel – Elec	1959–1960	13,792	*
730	S	Gas	1959–1960	292	****
	"	All-Fuel	1959–1960	28	*****
	"	LP	1959–1960	220	****
	"	Diesel – Pony	1959–1960	2,213	**
	"	Diesel – Elec	1959–1960	2,342	**

730	H	Gas	1959–1960	6	*****
	"	All-Fuel	1959–1960	4	*****
	"	LP	1959–1960	28	*****
	"	Diesel – Pony	1959–1960	7	*****
	"	Diesel – Elec	1959–1960	78	*****

Specifications

Model	G	GM	70	720/730	720/730 HC
Base price (1st year)	$2,600	$—	$3,000	$3,700	
Fuel	K	K	Gas	Gas	Diesel
Width (in)	84	84.5	86.6	86.6	74
Height to radiator (in)	61.5	65.9	65.6	88.25	101
Length (in)	135	137.6	136.25	135.25	148.3
Weight (lb)	4,400	5,100	6,035	6,790	8,470
Front tires/wheels (in)	24x5	6x16	6x16	6x16	7.5x20
Rear tires/wheels (in)	51.5x7	11x38	12x38	12x38	13.6x38
Fuel capacity (gal)	17	17	24.5	26.5	20
Coolant capacity (qt)	11	13	8.5	7.12	7
Gears forward/reverse	4/1	6/1	6/1	6/1	6/1

Engine / Power Data

	G	G	70	720	720
Fuel	Dist	Gas	Gas	Gas	Diesel
Nebraska Test No.	295	383	513	605	594
Nebraska Test year	11/15/37	6/5/47	5/15/53	11/6/56	9/18/56
Rated rpm	975	975	975	1,125	1,125
Bore and stroke (in)	6.12x7	6.12x7	5.87x7	6x6.37	6.12x6.37
Belt/PTO horsepower	35.91	38.10	50.4	59.12	58.84
Drawbar horsepower	27.63	34.49	44.2	53.05	53.66
Maximumimum pull	4,085	4,394	5,453	6,647	6547
Shipping weight (lb)	5,160	7,442	8,677	8,945	9,241

Parts Prices

MODEL	G		70		720		730	
	Low	High	Low	High	Low	High	Low	High
Air cleaner assembly					270		342	
Air cleaner intake stack	66	98			52	66	52	66
Amp gauge	20	70	20	50	20	50	20	50
Battery box/cover	50	95	100	180	100	180	100	130
Battery cable (set)	40							
Block								
Camshaft	145		167	249	167	235	235	
Carburetor	260	543	260	543	260	543	429	500
Carburetor float	23		25	28	25	28	25	28
Carburetor kit	17	30	20	71	20	71	20	71
Clutch drive disc			109	149	109	149	109	149
Clutch pulley cover	30	39	26	50	26	50	26	50
Clutch slider disc	56		56		56		56	
Connecting rod	150	195	150	175	159	175	175	
Crankshaft			588					
Cylinder head	510	767	451	509	376	475		
Dash								
Distributor	209	283	190	283	190	285	190	285
Distributor cap	30	55	15	30	17		17	

Part	C1	C2	C3	C4	C5	C6	C7	C8
Exhaust manifold	279							
Exhaust pipe	29	132	24	132	24	132	24	132
Fan assembly								
Fender	150	217	129	164	129	200	129	200
Flywheel			935	1054	935	1054	935	1054
Flywheel cover	118	150						
Fuel tank								
Generator	120	179	125	179	125	179	125	179
Grille screen	17	60	35	45	35	45	35	45
Grille with screen	350							
Headlight assembly	37	67	37	67	37	63	64	
Magneto	249	375						
Manifold (intake & exhaust)	155	300	210	236	182	250	182	250
Muffler	23	62	23	56	23	62	26	44
Overhaul kit (piston, rings, etc.)	475	553	509	699	509	699	509	699
Pan seat	35	55						
Piston								
Piston rings	199		199		149-289		149-289	
PTO shield	60	75	60	123	75	146	75	146
Radiator	308	316	316	401	316	401	316	401
Radiator cap	19	90	13	25	15	25	15	25
Radiator core	148	346	128	350	128	350	128	350
Seat cushion (bottom)	28	50	28	60	28	60	28	60
Sediment bowl	24	45	18	24	18	24	18	24
Spark plug wires (set)	11	17	11	13	11	13	11	13
Starter	220	389	125	399	125	547	125	547
Starter drive assembly	25	43	34	43				
Steering wheel	44	75	44	65	49	140	49	140
Three-point hitch	410	693	410	693	325	425	325	425
Toolbox	30	40	30	45	30	67	30	45
Voltage regulator	36	52	35	52	37	50	37	50
Water pump	157		110	157	110		110	
Weight, front			167		167		167	
Wheel bearings	69		69		69		69	
Wheel weights (405-lb set)			375		375		375	

Ratings
Collector's 5-Star Editions

Model	Fuel	#
GN Early Styled	All-Fuel	49
70HC	Diesel	44
70HC	LP	28
730S	All-Fuel	28
730H	LP	28
720H	LP	22
70HC	Gas	16
720H	All-Fuel	12
720H	D – Elec	9
730H	D – Pony	7
730H	Gas	6
720H	Gas	5
730H	All-Fuel	4

Average Sale Value 1995 to 2010 (Actual and Projected)

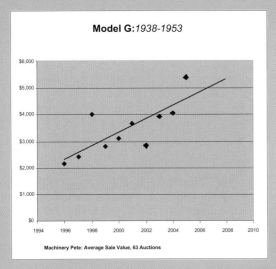

Model G: *1938-1953*

Machinery Pete: Average Sale Value, 63 Auctions

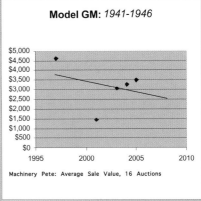

Model GM: *1941-1946*

Machinery Pete: Average Sale Value, 16 Auctions

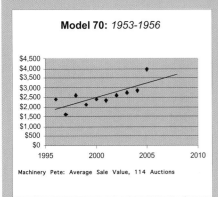

Model 70: *1953-1956*

Machinery Pete: Average Sale Value, 114 Auctions

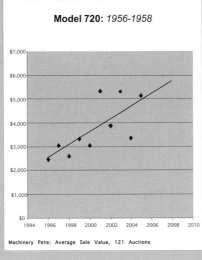

Model 720: *1956-1958*

Machinery Pete: Average Sale Value, 121 Auctions

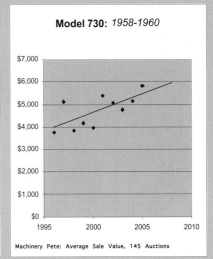

Model 730: *1958-1960*

Machinery Pete: Average Sale Value, 145 Auctions

A 1960 Model 430 Hi-Crop restored by Ron Jungmeyer. This tractor is one of about 180 that burned gasoline. *Ron Jungmeyer*

Chapter 6

Models H, M, 40, 320, 420, 330, 430, 435, 440

Ninety miles east of Waterloo, on the Mississippi River and closer to home base in Moline, Deere & Co. purchased 730 acres for a brand-new tractor factory on the northern outskirts of Dubuque, Iowa, in January 1945. Dubuque Tractor Works' first two-cylinder was a Model M, completed on March 12, 1947. A month later, the new Model M began arriving at dealers' showrooms. During the next 13 years, the Dubuque assembly lines built approximately 230,000 two-cylinder tractors in about 70 model variations. Dubuque's tractors were smaller than Waterloo's Model B, but their roots went back to the Depression era.

At the time, horses were still the big competitors to tractors. The new row-crop tractors were doing well for sales on midsize and large farms, but the little Model B was a bit large for thousands of small farms that relied on a single team of horses. A slightly smaller tractor in the right price range could generate thousands of tractor sales.

In 1936, Deere directors commissioned the design of a small tractor. It would replace a single team of horses at a price that small farms could afford. In time, this effort led to the development of two families of small tractors that were built at Waterloo and in two other cities. The first family, the Model Y and its successors, is the subject of Chapter 7. That family came into production in 1937 at Moline. It was the smallest two-cylinder tractor built by Deere and was built in Waterloo for about 10 years until the new Dubuque facility opened in 1947. Waterloo began building the second family of small-farm tractors in 1939 with introduction of the Model H. In 1947, the small-tractor lines at both Waterloo and Dubuque were shut down when the new Dubuque facility opened.

Model H

John Deere introduced its smallest Waterloo tractor, the Model H, in January 1939. It looked like a miniature Model B, and at 2,054 pounds, it was about 700 pounds lighter than the original 1934 Model B. It could do two-row work on most fields. At $600, the price was affordable. It turned out to be well suited to a second market. Larger farms that already had a row-crop tractor liked the Model H for its ability to do light jobs at low cost. In the long green tractor line at dealerships, it became a filler tractor between the Model B and the even smaller Model L. Over an eight-year production run beginning in 1939, Deere built approximately 60,000 Model H tractors, including three variations. It was introduced as a styled tractor, although a handful of experimental predecessors were unstyled before being rebuilt as a styled H.

The Model H was, and remains, a neat little tractor as long as you're not in a hurry. The Model H was anything but nimble and quick. A foot-operated governor override would let it go double-speed, up to 7.5 miles per hour, on good roads. The Model H was only available with 32-inch rubber tires. When it was time to brake, there were no bull gears. The brakes on this little tractor applied directly to the axle.

The Model H had a new engine, which was the smallest two-cylinder horizontal engine ever put on a John Deere tractor. It only displaced about 100 cubic inches, but raced along at 1,400 rpm. On the Nebraska test, it kicked out a little less than 12.5 horsepower on the drawbar and nearly 15 horsepower on the belt. A camshaft drive for the belt pulley, rather than crankshaft, allowed the increased engine speed. However, it also meant the belt pulley operated counterclockwise.

Burning cheap distillate, the little engine set a fuel economy record. Rear tread was adjustable, from 44 to 84 inches. According to historian J. R. Hobbs, the Model H "was perhaps the most versatile and adaptable tractor in its class, despite the claims made by Ford-Ferguson for its 9N. Even more versatility was made possible by ordering a PTO, priced at a most reasonable $18."[7]

Deere provided two surprises for the Model H line for 1941. One was hydraulic Power Lift. It was driven from the engine governor shaft and provided live hydraulic power to operate one or two hydraulic cylinders. The second was electric starting and lighting, beginning in mid-1941 at serial number 27000, even though the small engine was easy to start. Many modifications were made during the production years.

Farmers liked the narrow, tapered hood as they looked ahead on the little tractor that replaced a horse or team of horses. The tractor provided great visibility, and it could pull a wide choice of implements. Many implements were developed to work with the Model H, including plows, tillers, cultivators, planters, hoe, rake, binder, harvester, mower, and more. Production was shut down from May 1942 to April 1943. The Model H was cancelled in February 1947.

There were three variations of the Model H. The second and third variations are very rare tractors. The Model HN was the first of the variations, and production started in April 1940. The HN had a single front wheel and was excellent for narrow row-crops. Over seven years, Waterloo built less than 1,000 HN tractors.

The Model HNH had the HN single front wheel, but the rear wheels were 6 inches taller and gave it a

This Michigan beauty is a 1940 HN with PTO and manual start. It looks like it was built yesterday and delivered this morning.
John Nelson

nose-down-to-the-ground appearance. Deere built 37 of the HNH tractors.

The Model HWH was the third variation. Deere only built about 125 of these high and wide tractors at Waterloo between February 1941 and March 1942. They were all sent to vegetable growers in California and are known as the California Hi-Crop H. It had 6 inches more ground clearance than the Model H, front and rear. Axle width could be adjusted to 68 inches wide on the front and 84 inches on the back. These are eye-catching and extremely valuable tractors. Sales of four have been reported since 2001, with three in a range from $19,000 to $43,000.

As an investment, Model H tractors generally have increased in value at a modest pace. Compared to Dubuque tractors, Waterloo's smallest tractors are still available at a reasonable price in the market, although they don't come up very often. At auction, reports indicate the value has increased about 50 percent over the past 10 years. The typical Model H in 2005 sold at auction for about $3,000, compared to $2,000 a decade earlier. A short car trailer can haul one home from an auction.

Model H Buyers' Guide

"We rebuild a lot of governors. The governor is the weakest point on the H tractors. If you have to go through the governor, gears, bearings, everything, you're going to spend $1,500. That's why they get salvaged. The bearings are $70 each, and it takes four. Gears are $400, and used gears don't exist. This is all new stuff that has to be built. And they're very difficult to set up. They set up like a ring and pinion on a car, and not just anybody can do that. You've got to press the gears off and set them back. It's a big deal. Most people don't have the ability to do all that work. " — Melanie Sharp, Sharp's Antique Tractor Works, Fair Grove, Missouri

"Look at the rims. Many farmers put calcium chloride in the rims and it ate the rims out. You can get new outer rims, but not new centers. Then, look at the sheet metal. Hoods are extremely hard to find. I say you're better off to pay $2,000 or $3,000 for a good tractor so you don't have to do too much." — Charles Lindstrom, Elwood, Kansas

"The radiator pulley is something to look at. I never put a tractor back together with a used radiator core out of it. It's a job to replace a core on a radiator on an H. You've got to

The Model HWH is a rare bird that was built in Waterloo for California's vegetable growers. Only 126 were built in 1941 and early 1942. It was a compact version of the BWH. *Bruce Keller*

take off your grilles and hood, the steering shaft comes out and sometimes the pan shaft in order to get the radiator out. Then you can scratch everything up so you're better off to spend $165 on a radiator core and some gaskets and just replace it." — Charles Lindstrom, Elwood, Kansas

"Better than money in the bank. I'm serious. You can't buy a stock or a bond that will pay you the time-weighted average that a John Deere will." — Charles Lindstrom, Elwood, Kansas

"There's a lot of secrets or things to know. Take a leaky oil pump. If you don't use one of my gaskets or one of John Deere's in the very bottom of it, there's such close tolerance that you won't have any oil pressure. If you put the correct gasket in there, you can turn the oil pressure up or down wherever you want it.

"One thing you want to watch on an H: they got water inside [the engine] and they froze and broke. The stress point was in the belly, and there's no way to weld it or successfully patch it. I've had a lot of them that way." — Charles Lindstrom, Elwood, Kansas

This 1949 MC was built soon after Deere acquired the Lindeman factory in Yakima, Washington, and the rights to use its crawler track system. Prior to that, Deere supplied the Model BO chassis for mounting by Lindeman. The MC was a cooperative project between Dubuque and Yakima until 1952. It had three rollers for the track. *Leon Rumpf*

Model M

The new Dubuque, Iowa, John Deere factory completed its first tractor, a Model M, on March 12, 1947. It went on to build 87,000 more Model M series tractors and crawlers during the next six years, as well as several other tractor lines. The Model M was a very successful tractor line and sturdy enough to stay at work for the next 50 years. As a collector's piece, the Model M has mostly been ignored by collectors. It

is not rare, although there are a few highly collectable units. It is a small field tractor that makes a good beginner project at a reasonable starting price.

The Model M had been developed during the war years. Like the Model H at Waterloo, it was to be smaller than the Model B family but larger than the successful Model L/LA family coming out of Moline. It was distinguished from the Model H family as a slightly larger tractor with the latest bells

This industrial version of the Model M has been correctly restored. The MI tractors are even shorter and lower than the Model M, and are in short supply. It's a real eye-catcher when restored. *Ron Jungmeyer*

The Model MT tricycle front had a new dual Touch-O-Matic split rockshaft that enabled independent control of front- and rear-mounted implements. This 1951 MT gas version is set up with the MT-200 cultivator. *Kenny Earman*

This is a 1954 Model 40 standard gas version that Dubuque introduced in 1953 as a Number series replacement for Model M tractors. *Kenny Earman*

and whistles of 1940s technology and a completely new engine. It had to compete against Ford's supersuccessful 9N that was introduced in 1941.

Two big differences between Waterloo and Dubuque tractors should be noted here. The Dubuque tractors had less casting material and were lighter. Stripped down in a restoration shop, a Waterloo tractor still looks like a tractor because of the large casting pieces. A Dubuque tractor is a loose collection of bolts and pipes and brackets. Another difference is that the Dubuque-built tractor transmission is engaged with a foot clutch. The Waterloo tractors all used a hand clutch. Learning to operate a hand clutch safely can be a challenge for a younger collector. "As far as moving around, they're awkward," one restorer said. "To back up, you're turning your head backwards while throwing your arm forward. You're fighting your whole body to do this!"[8]

Touch-O-Matic, also nicknamed the "Liquid Brain," was introduced with the 1947 Model M. Engineers developed a new hydraulics system for the new tractor and mounted a hydraulic pump on the front of the engine to provide live hydraulic power. It controlled a cylinder that operated a

rockshaft mounted at the rear of the tractor. The rockshaft controlled a drawbar that could pivot up and down using chains or solid links. Like Powr-Trol on the Waterloo tractors, it enabled precise positioning. It worked very well and was kept in production as an option through 1960.

A new attachment system was developed for implements. Most had a Quick-Tatch system so the operator could back into a waiting implement, put in one or two pins, and drive away with it. Tillage implements could be leveled with a special yoke under the tractor.

The new Dubuque engine had overhead vertical valves as opposed to the horizontal vales built for Waterloo tractors. It generated a maximum rating of just over 18 horsepower on the drawbar and nearly 20.5 horsepower on the belt with virtually the same displacement as Waterloo's Model H engine and cranked over at 1,650 rpm. It burned gasoline and had an improved four-speed transmission.

In terms of maintenance, the new Dubuque tractors were excellent. People with long experience in restoration say that Dubuque tractors were well built with strong components. Pieces didn't wear out. However, they did have a problem with

A Model 40T row-crop tractor has been restored to showroom shape. It was available with single, double, or wide front axles. *Ron Jungmeyer*

leaks. They could leak anywhere, although the area around the hydraulic system and hitch seemed to be the worst.

Two versions of the Model M are recorded in *John Deere Tractors & Equipment, Vol. 1.* The standard Model M was built to cultivate one row. It had even wheel spacing, front and back. The MT was a taller tricycle version with a single front wheel and wide axle and was built from 1949 to 1952. It cultivated two rows and had two-row equipment. The MC, a crawler version with three track rollers, was built in the same period. Dubuque built about 30,500 of the MT tractors and 10,500 crawlers. A handful of the MT tractors had the height of the MT but a wide front end, similar to a hi-crop tractor.

A third version was the MI. Deere built about 1,000 units of the MI, which was an industrial version that was a bit shorter and lower and painted a bright, solid yellow or orange.

Apparently, an orchard version was discussed but never built at the factory. However, at least one dealership modified a few Model M tractors to an orchard configuration. At least five are known to exist.

The Model M market value has risen very slowly in comparison to most other tractors discussed in this book. Highest values recorded are $6,100 at a 2005 auction for a Model M and $5,100 for an overhauled Model MT the same year. Four other auction sales reports for the year show a value range of $3,000 to $3,500. These were well above the few reports from 10 years earlier, and that's probably as much as can be said accurately from the available data.

Model M Buyers' Guide

"A lot of guys called them the Dubuque Dribblers. They said you never have to worry about them being rusty because they had enough leaks to keep them well oiled so they wouldn't rust. You can put seals in those lift arms and they'll leak again after three or four months. When you buy one, you know the lift arm is going to be leaking by the rockshaft.

"The lift system on Dubuque tractors was different. It was called Touch-O-Matic and it worked off a hydraulic pump on the engine. You could have a dual Touch-O-Matic so your left and right lift arms operated separate. You could raise your front cultivators separate from your rear cultivators. It was live, where with the Waterloo tractors, you had to engage the clutch and have the transmission gears turning for the live to work. The live would work on the Dubuque tractors whether the clutch was in or out because it had its own hydraulic pump on the engine." — Malcolm McIntyre, White House, Tennessee

"The Ms that I've run across, the front ends were a little bit weak on every one of them. Nearly every one has the front end beefed up or it's been broken and rewelded. They're not real strong where the main pivot pin is under the radiator.

"They leaked at just about every seal! Even when you put a new one back together, it's just hard to keep them from leaking. They got better as the 40s and 420s came along, but still they had quite a bit of problems with rear axle seals and the final drives leaking. That's about the worst thing I can say about those Dubuque tractors.

"[Dubuque tractors] were quite a bit lighter weight. Nearly all of them had wheel weights on the front if they did any pulling. They were real light in the front end. If you drive one that has no weights at all, if you pop the clutch a little too fast, the front end will want to hop for you." — Kenny Earman, Early Iron Restoration, Mt. Pleasant, Texas

"The M just didn't have the three-point hitch. That hurt it then and still hurts it today. You can't do much with it.

"For Ms the wheels are rotted out, the front wheels are busted, the front hubcaps are broke off, and the front axles are wore out. Tie rod ends are broke or wore plumb out. Transmissions are typically fairly good in them, with the exception of the PTO. If they've been run on a Bush Hog, they're not worth a thing. The tractor will keep running [after]

The very first production unit of the Model 40 Hi-Crop, an all-fuel version completed on August 27, 1954, is now in a museum collection. *Bruce Keller*

The 40C crawler replaced the MC in production. It had a track frame with four or five rollers. This particular machine was built in 1954. *John Detmer*

it hits something that stops the Bush Hog and something will give in there. It's typically the transmission or PTO shaft.

"Probably the worst part on Ms is the sheet metal. The sheet metal is typically beat all to hell because the nose stuck out farther than the front wheels did, and having that wide front end on it, people run into stuff. Most of the Ms around here, if there was a tree within 40 miles they hit it 18 times in one day.

"Ms are bad about busting heads and blocks. New heads are available, but blocks are not. Hydraulics and brakes aren't too bad, just a pain to rebuild." — Donnie Sharp, Sharp's Antique Tractor Works, Fair Grove, Missouri

Model 40

As it had with bigger tractors like the Models A, B, G, and R, Deere chose to replace the popular Model M series with a Numbered version, the Model 40. It was introduced in November 1952 as a 1953 model. Deere wanted, and received, improved operator comfort and convenience, a three-point hitch that would work, more horsepower, good fuel economy, and more in the Model 40.

Styling was updated to resemble the Models 50 and 60 that had been introduced a few months earlier. The Model 40 had more space on the operator's platform; a deep, cushioned seat; a new three-point hitch with an exclusive load and depth control; Touch-O-Matic hydraulics; and a wide range of implement options.

Inside, the Model 40 retained the Model M engine. However, bore and stroke were squared up to 4x4 inches, compression increased to 6.5:1, and rpm was boosted to 1,850. The combination gave this little tractor 15 percent more horsepower than the M series. Four months later, an all-fuel option for the engine became available for an extra $36.

About 49,000 Model 40 tractors in seven variations were built by the end of the last production run in October 1955. That's enough variation to generate a collection.

The top three in the Model 40 family are the utility, crawler, and tricycle versions. With gasoline engines, there were about 5,000 of the utility versions built, twice as many crawlers, and more than 17,000 tricycles. However, there were fewer than 850 of the all-fuel-option units built. Proportions stay the same with the less popular variations, the hi-crop, standard, special, and two-row utility (W). Rarest is the all-fuel 40 special (V), where fewer than five are recorded.

Here's how they were promoted at the time in John Deere literature:

40 standard—The two-plow general purpose tractor for speedy, economical work on all tillage jobs, mowing, hauling, and one-row planting and cultivating in corn, cotton, tobacco, and similar crops.

40 tricycle—The two-plow general-purpose tractor for all-around farm work that furnishes two-row capacity in corn, cotton, [and] tobacco; and four- or six-row capacity in beans, beets, lettuce, and similar crops.

40 hi-crop—The two-plow tractor with extra-high clearance (32 inches under the tractor) and wide wheel spacings for cultivating tall, bushy, or high-bedded crops.

40 with single front wheel—This model is the same as the 40 tricycle except for the single front wheel, which provides extra clearance in narrow-spaced rows. A favorite with vegetable growers everywhere.

Charles Wiman, a president of Deere & Co., had this Model 40 standard sent to his personal ranch in California. It's equipped with front and rear wheel weights. *Bruce Keller*

40 with wide front axle—This is another variation of the tricycle model for growers who want an extra-wide wheel adjustment on the front axle, as well as the rear.

40 crawler—This rugged, highly maneuverable track-type tractor is used on many farms throughout the world, and is a favorite for light logging and contracting jobs. Pulls three-plow bottoms. Available with either four- or five-roller track frame.

40 two-row utility—It retains the low, stable, overall design of the 40 utility . . . but has increased crop clearance and wider wheel treads to straddle and cultivate two rows of corn, cotton, beans, peanuts, and similar crops.

Garden-variety Model 40 tractors are the only group in the John Deere two-cylinder tractor production to show a

flat line in auction value trend over the past decade. They were a high-production tractor in the 1950s and are 20 years younger than the high-production As and Bs of the 1930s. Considering the number built, they show up less frequently at auction than one might expect. Considering the age, performance, number produced, and durability, they may not yet be as ready for putting into collection dress as others. For those that do come up at auction, the flat line absolute value is around $3,300, with a range of about $300. That's well above the Model H or M series, although they have been gainingsome ground.

On the other hand, low production variations of the 40 have high value. A restored all-fuel 40W sold in 2003 for

This is a rare Model 320 Special, which is also known as the 320V. It has standard tread and the slant steering wheel. *Bruce Keller*

more than $13,000. It was reported as one of 60 built. In 2005, a 40V exceeded $6,000 on the auction block and a loaded 1953 40T went for $7,500.

Model 40 Buyers' Guide

"On the M and on the early 40 standard, the steering would get a lot of play; you had to rebuild them. But that's the only weak point I know. There really wasn't much for weak points on the Dubuque tractors.

"I've never had any trouble with getting parts for them. I restored a little 40T. The first time around, from Deere, I ordered a total of 175 parts [including gaskets and nickel-dime parts], and I got 72 of them! You can't buy something

like a casting, but the things that keep it running, you can get today from the dealer. You try that with any other brand that's 50 years old." — Ron Jungmeyer, Jungmeyer Tractor Restoration Service, Russellville, Missouri

"I would definitely go with at least the 40 series or above [if I was starting a collection], just because they're a much more usable tractor. If you want to collect one to parade and use, they're so much more useful than an M because they all have three-point, and there's so many attachments you can use them with. The M was very limited. You had to have equipment that was made especially for an M or MT two-point type of hitch setup." — Kenny Earman, Early Iron Restoration, Mt. Pleasant, Texas

Model 320

Deere introduced the 20 series tractors for 1956 as new replacements for the early Numbered series with one exception, the Model 320. It was completely new, without a predecessor. While the 20 series generally had a 20 percent power increase, the 320 moved into the long green line at the bottom end as a low-power tractor. It came out of Dubuque and was patterned after the Model M. It weighed about the same as the M or 40, had the M engine, and was priced a little higher than the Model 40. In addition to the basic Model, the 320 was offered in two variations targeted for vegetable growers and very small farms.

The Model 320 series found its niche, mostly in the South, but it was never a big seller. Today, collectors have a special liking for it and for the Model 330 that replaced it. As a series, they are at the top of the two-cylinder price list in today's market.

Complete production of the Model 320 was approximately 3,080 tractors, ending with the 1958 model. They were built in two distinct phases.

For most of its production history, the Model 320 steering wheel was straight up and down relative to the operator. That was phase one, with approximately 2,560 tractors. Phase two came late in the production as the 30 series was

A 1959 Model 330 standard gas is the smallest member of the 30 series tractors in this Canadian collection. *Elmer Friesen*

A 30 series collection owned by the Friesen family in southern Manitoba. *Elmer Friesen*

being prepared. Approximately the last 520 of the Model 320 tractors came out with a slanted dash and slanted steering wheel. These were much more comfortable for operators and are in high demand among collectors. About 60 percent of Model 320 production was the basic model, but there were two variations and some other differences during the production run.

The 320S (standard) boasted a crop clearance of 21 inches. It appealed to growers of peanuts, vegetables, berries, and tobacco. The 320 Southern Special was a variation of the 320S that was made for a handful of farms in Louisiana and Texas. The 60 to 70 Southern Specials produced had even higher clearance for use in certain vegetable crops.

The 320U (utility) had a lower stance than the basic Model 320. It had shorter spindles in front and geared, off-set rear axles (rather than direct-drive axles) that produced a tractor that was about 5 inches lower. Its special appeal was

for orchard operators, people in the mowing business, and those working in confined areas. Deere built about half as many of the little 320 utility tractors as it did standards, so the 320U is worth more today.

A few Model 320 tractors were purchased for industrial uses, like highway work, and were painted bright orange or yellow.

The Model 320 had the same engine as the Model 40 with a bore and stroke of 4x4 inches. Another small group of less than 20 tractors had the all-fuel engine.

Popular production features were retained on the 320. These included disk brakes, push-button starting, the new Float-Ride seat that was adjustable for the operator's weight, Touch-O-Matic live hydraulics, and the load-compensating three-point hitch called Load-and-Depth Control. Early in production, the crankshaft and rods on the Model 320 were upgraded to those used on the Model 420.

This is an early, all-green 1956 version of the Model 420 standard with an extended rear axle. In two years the 420 went through three phases. *John Detmer*

This all-green 1958 Model 420 standard, which is in its original condition, is ready to go to work.
Dave Hadam

Here is another original 1958 Model 420, the T version, with an M-20 mower mounted on the right side. *Dixon Somerville*

This is an unusual 1956 420T LP tractor with an adjustable wide front axle. *John Detmer*

Sheet metal on the 20 series was nearly the same as on the series it replaced. However, the 20 series sported a new, flashy paint job with horizontal and vertical bands of bold yellow on the sides of the hood.

Anyone who had the foresight to collect a few of the Model 320 tractors back in the 1990s could make good money on the investment today. In 10 years, the value has more than doubled. Out of 12 auction sales recorded in 2004 and 2005 for the 320 series tractors, only two sold for well under $10,000. The high end was $20,000 for a Southern Special. Most clustered just over $10,000. This is based on a small number of reported sales. The number of reported sales shot up in 2005, which is perhaps an aberration or a sign that some 320 owners are ready to let go at today's prices.

Model 320 Buyers' Guide

"I guess because the 330s [are] so high, people are saying they'll buy a 320. Now the 320s have gone crazy. I just sold a 320 for $10,000. Ten years ago, that was unreal. I used to buy them for $2,500. I think that's related to the fact they're almost a 330 and guys can't afford a 330." — Malcolm McIntyre, White House, Tennessee

"The availability of the 320 was nearly none. If you're going to collect the whole 20 or 30 series, you better start with that one because it's the hardest one to find and they bring big bucks now. I think [they] didn't sell many because they were such a small tractor. People were wanting bigger and better at that period. The 320 was pretty much like a little M." — Kenny Earman, Early Iron Restoration, Mt. Pleasant, Texas

Model 420

One of the most popular small, row-crop tractors of the 1950s was Dubuque's Model 420. It replaced the popular Model 40 for 1956, but with significant improvements. Deere sold about 47,000 of these little tractors, similar to the production of the Model 40 and Model M.

The Model 420 was the first of the 20 series to be introduced. It actually came out in late 1955, about eight months ahead of schedule. The others emerged in the summer of 1956.

Early Model 420 tractors were painted all green and are called phase one tractors. Phase two Model 420 tractors had the new, flashy yellow-and-green paint job. Starting with phase two, Deere offered a Direction Reverser option for all Model 420 tractors except the hi-crop.

The Model 420 had 20 percent more power. The bore had been increased a quarter inch, giving it a 113-ci displacement, and it cranked over at 1,850 rpm. The little vertical, two-cylinder gasoline engine produced 29 horsepower on the belt, which is more than the Model B and essentially equal to the Model 50. It was also considerably lighter than the late styled B or the Model 50.

Detail view of the 420 LP fuel system and steering wheel. There is no room to slant this dash or wheel! *Gary Crain*

The 420 was mainly produced with a gasoline engine, but about 5,000 burned either all-fuel or LP gas. Production of the all-fuel or LP gas units in some of the subgroups was less than 10 tractors, making them exceptionally rare and valuable.

Dubuque built eight versions of the Model 420 tractor on its assembly lines. Collectors can find five or six of the

The Model 420 Hi-Crop all-fuel tractor was built for export to South Africa. *Bruce Keller*

versions fairly easily, but two were low-production lines. The 420V (special) was a unique version. They were built to straddle vegetable crops grown on high seedbeds, but were only half as high as the 420 Hi-Crop. Fewer than 90 were built. The 420I (special utility) was modified for light industry applications. About 250 were built. The 420T (row-crop) had dual front wheels with narrow spacing. The 420S (standard) had an adjustable wide front axle and 22 inches of clearance. The 420H (hi-crop) had a short phase-three edition. The steering wheels on these units were slanted and made of plastic rather than steel. The 420U (utility) had an adjustable wide front axle and 17 inches of clearance. The 420W (two-row utility) had a low, wide front and adjustable width. The 420C (crawler) was available in either four- or five-roller track configurations, like the 40C. With five rollers, it was longer and less maneuverable, but it had better flotation and stability. It was beefed up to handle chores in construction and forestry and had an all-fuel option.

Detail of the decal scheme on Deere tractors built in the United States for export purposes. *Bruce Keller*

A Model 430 crawler in the storage area of a private Ontario showroom. *Gerry Dubrick*

This Model 430T row-crop was restored to pristine condition. *Ron Jungmeyer*

Detail view of the Float-Ride seat, correct Touch-O-Matic decal, and control lever. *John Dietz*

Values in the 420 series have trended upwards over the past decade, but there is a wide range of models, conditions, situations, locations, and auctions. Like the Model 40, its predecessor, it was a high-production tractor and has survived very well over five decades. It would be safe to say the value is up 50 percent. The record set in 2005 was $42,500 for an LP gas, phase three, 420 standard that was reported as one of only 23 ever produced. Less than two weeks later, two more 420 garden-variety standards sold with a combined value of $10,000.

Model 420 Buyers' Guide

"An M, a 40, and a 420 look basically the same from a distance. The engine was basically the same. They increased the displacement and the compression ratio and things, but it was still the same basic tractor from 1947 through 1960. On the 20 and 30, the sheet metal is the only difference."
— Malcolm McIntyre, White House, Tennessee

"Crawlers have really gained quite a bit of popularity the last few years. If you have a nice one in the 420s or 430s, they bring pretty good money now, especially if you have a good blade. There's not a lot of them, either. A lot of those crawlers even had three-point hitches. You wouldn't think people would do much plowing with one, but I guess in certain areas, like out in

This is a 1958 Model 430 standard gas tractor that is part of a collection in Manitoba. *John Dietz*

California with those hillsides, they used them quite a bit for stability." — Kenny Earman, Early Iron Restoration, Mt. Pleasant, Texas

Model 330

Collectors who have been looking for the gem in the haystack may want to stop here and think. The Model 330 is the most sought-after modern two-cylinder John Deere tractor. Period.

Like the M and 320, in its time it was offered as a low-cost tractor for small farms and small jobs that didn't need much power. The list price in 1960 was $2,200, which is slightly more than the value of the serial number tag in today's market.

It had the basic Model M vertical engine with 4x4-inch bore and stroke and running at 1,650 rpm. At 21.5 horsepower, it did manage a bit more horsepower on the belt. Mechanically, it was identical to the phase two Model 320 with slant dash and steering wheel. Paintwise, the Model 330 had the brighter, streamlined 30 series paint scheme with fewer bends in the sheet metal. It had lots of options, including an air precleaner, a rear exhaust, and an exhaust silencer for use where engine noise was objectionable.

The Model 330 was built in only two versions, standard or utility, with only a four-speed transmission and gasoline engine. The standard was an early precision farming tractor

Detail view of the slanted black dash on the Model 430.
John Dietz

A worm's-eye view of the Model 430 from the rear. *John Dietz*

for crops that needed precision work. For the big farm, it was the handyman tractor. The utility version was a good, economical, all-purpose tractor.

In retrospect, the Models 330 and 430 were a little too close in size and price. The 430 had about 20 percent more power and cost only $300 more. It outsold the 330 by more than 12 to 1. Today, the 330 has more than twice the market value for collectors, even though the two models are quite similar.

Dubuque built the Model 330S (standard) between July 1958 and February 1960. Production was less than 840 tractors and hardly enough to go around among the number of collectors today. The Model 330 utility is even harder to find. Dubuque only built about 250 of these tractors. Post-factory, a few 330s were converted into what would have been the 330V (special) with parts from a 40V or 420V. It seems that a few industrial units also were built on a special order with a red paint scheme. Deere's Industrial Division also sold a few that were painted all yellow.

The market value for Model 330 tractors reflects demand rather than number built. In the overall John Deere

two-cylinder production, there are dozens of instances where production was lower than 840 tractors in a given model. A truly rare tractor, a Collector's Edition, should have a production number lower than 100. In fact, there are quite a few examples of configurations where the factory only recorded production of 2 to 10 tractors.

Other factors in the market are durability and size. In this case, the bigger the piece of iron, the less likely it will be valued for anything but iron. The Model 330 is a small tractor, although it is larger than a garden tractor. It's about as small as they come in reference to self-propelled field-crop machinery. It's easy to store and haul, and relatively easy to handle in a shop. As one restoration guy pointedly asked, "What would you rather have, a 1974 Impala or a 1974 Corvette?"

Durability matters. A tractor that doesn't need much attention and does its job tends to stay on the farm a long

This Model 430 standard is ready for restoration. It's small enough for a project in a two-car garage. *Dave Hadam*

time as a working machine. Many of these 1950s tractors are still "in their chore clothes" and working for a living. In this case, Deere made about 1,100 Model 330 tractors in total. These were very durable machines, staying in chore clothes long enough to become collector's items rather than migrating to fence rows and salvage yards. It is entirely possible that 800 or more of these tractors still exist.

The 330s were small, durable, operator-friendly tractors on small farms. They were relied upon, but weren't abused or abandoned compared to many larger row-crop tractors. They

Immaculate restoration work has been done on this 1959 Model 435 diesel with an adjustable front axle. *Bill Peets*

could be a "first tractor" for the next generation to learn on. It isn't unreasonable to estimate that many collectors would like to own one of these tractors, and it's not a surprise that the value has soared as collectors have aged toward retirement years.

Very few Model 330 tractors come to the auction block. Observers have recorded seven sales in four years to the end of 2005. The lowest price was $15,250. The high price, recorded in June 2005, was $23,000. If you get the opportunity, it looks like this is a safe place to invest some cash for a while.

Model 330 Buyers' Guide

"They sold a 330U down in Georgia a couple weeks ago for $30,000—just a tractor in its work clothes. When I first started fooling with tractors, I bought a 330 for $6,000 and I thought I'd paid too much. It wasn't no time before they were up to $10,000

"It costs as much to restore a John Deere B that's going to be worth $3,500 as it costs to restore a 330 that's going to be worth $20,000. So if you want to do one for money, looking at what it's going to be worth, you want to do a high-price tractor." — Malcolm McIntyre, White House, Tennessee

These hood panels have been well restored and properly painted. The proper decals are applied with the correct placement. *John Dietz*

This is a substantial Category III hitch and PTO on the relatively small Model 435. *John Dietz*

Model 430

The Model 430 was the culmination of more than 40 years of two-cylinder tractor-building experience in the company. It was introduced in 1958, along with others in the 30 series. Mechanically, the 430 was identical to the late slant-steer 420. It used the same vertical inline two-cylinder engine as its predecessor, with a 7:1 compression ratio and producing 29 horsepower at the belt. A four-speed transmission was standard, although a five-speed could be ordered.

It had some additional instruments; the new, more comfortable seat; and the hydraulic three-point hitch that was

The view from this angle shows the spin-out rear hubs for adjustable tread width. *John Dietz*

Detail view of the five-speed transmission lever and housing. *John Dietz*

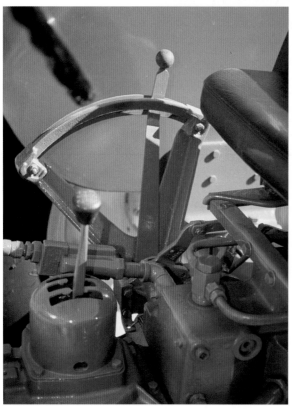

used on the Model 320. The 430 also had either regular or heavy-duty fender options.

The shuttle-type Direction Reverser system, introduced on the late 420, was an important option on the Model 430. It could be installed at the factory or in the field. It permitted the use of any forward gears for backing up by stopping the tractor, pushing in the clutch, and moving a lever forward or backward. It was a huge help for front-end loader work. For collectors, Direction Reverser is an asset. Reasonable value for this item today is $500 to $1,000.

Deere built nearly 15,000 tractors in seven versions of the 430 series between July 1958 and February 1960. A small portion of the 430 fleet used all-fuel or LP gas instead of gasoline. Direction Reverser was not available on the LP gas models or on tractors with a live PTO.

The 430W (row-crop utility) was the most popular. Deere built nearly 6,000 of these. The Model 430T (tricycle, convertible) was second in production. Deere sold 3,250 of these with a choice of three front ends: single wheel, two-wheel tricycle, or wide.

On the rare side, about 210 were built as hi-crop units. About 70 were built into forklifts known as the 430U (early) or 430 F-3 (late), and another 60-plus were built as the 430V

(special). Deere also built more than 2,000 of the 430C crawler-type tractors.

A special high-altitude version was available so some of these tractors could work at altitudes above 4,000 feet. These engines had a high-compression cylinder head to compensate for the reduced air pressure at high elevations.

The Model 430 has a wide range of value at auction, similar to the Model 420 and 40 tractors that came before it. The garden-variety 430 has increased in value probably a third to a half in 10 years, but there are exceptions. Most were purchased for around $4,500 in 2005. Relatively rare hi-crop versions sold for $13,000 to $23,000.

Model 430 Buyers' Guide

"The low-number tractors is what people want, and they pay big money. I just sold a 430W. It was just a nice old tractor and it went for $3,700. If it had been a 430U or S, it would have brought a whole lot more

"Nothing will add to the value of a Dubuque tractor like power steering. It will add $1,500 to $2,000 to the value of the tractor. They go crazy over tractors with power steering. A nice restored 430 that's going to bring maybe $5,000 to $6,000 will bring $7,000 if it's got power steering."
— Malcolm McIntyre, White House, Tennessee

Model 435

The last two-cylinder tractor added to the line in 1959, the Model 435, is a very special tractor among Johnny Poppers. For one thing, it isn't technically a Johnny Popper. It raced along with a different style of two-cylinder diesel engine made by General Motors Corporation. It had a 53-ci displacement on each cylinder, a tremendous compression ratio of 17:1, and a supercharger. The engine was known as the Detroit 2-53 Diesel. It produced almost 33 horsepower on the PTO belt and 28.4 horsepower at the drawbar at 1,850 rpm.

More important, for Johnny Popper collectors, the 435 sounded very different. The lore on the true sound of a Johnny Popper is deep and a little mystical. Most collectors have a special love for that slow, deep, throaty sound, and some can identify the model by the sound of the particular engine. However, the sound of a Model 435 speaks more to the heart of a logger or biker.

"It's like a two-stroke engine. It fired on every stroke," says Malcolm McIntyre, a collector and restoration specialist. "The 435 diesel is referred to many times as like a chain saw with hemorrhoids."

Engines for both the Waterloo Boy Model LA and the Dubuque Model 435 had evenly spaced power strokes with two horizontally opposed cylinders. All of the "true" Johnny

Poppers have power strokes that cause them to fire on a 180- to 540-degree schedule.

The Model 435 was essentially a Model 430 row-crop utility tractor with different footwear and a diesel engine. At the time, with the New Generation tractors just around the corner, it was more economical for Deere to borrow a good two-cylinder diesel already in production than to develop a whole new engine.

The first Model 435 was built on March 31, 1959, and the last of 4,626 units was built on February 29, 1960. Deere had an export market for this tractor. Some 371 units of the 435 were assembled in Monterey, Mexico, for the Latin American market. Although it isn't covered in this book, collectors should be aware that the 435 was brought back into production in 1963 as the Model 445 built in Rosario, Argentina. They continued in production until 1972.

As a power unit, the Model 435 shared the same chassis and features as the Model 430W. The 430 had a four-speed transmission with a five-speed option. Starting the 435's diesel engine became a problem when the temperature fell below 50 degrees Fahrenheit. It was easy to overcome by plumbing a heater into the cooling system.

The Farm and Industrial Equipment Institute and the American Society of Agricultural Engineers, along with the Society of Automotive Engineers, set up standards in 1958 for PTOs and hitches. The Model 435 was the first John Deere tested by the University of Nebraska under the new 540- to 1,000-rpm PTO standards.

Attention to detail takes a lot of time, but it results in a good restoration. *John Dietz*

Model 435 Buyers' Guide

"I took one 430 out of a fence row and was going to fix it but I didn't. It was just a basket case. The guy gave it to me to get it out of his fence row. I put it on eBay as a parts tractor. This guy bought it for $600 for parts to fix his 435. He changed his mind when he discovered the 430 was an all-fuel. He was enough of a John Deere guy to know it was worth a lot of money, so he restored it and took it to a collector's auction and it brought $10,000. That would be two or three years ago this fall." — Malcolm McIntyre, White House, Tennessee

Model 435. *John Dietz*

At auction, $6,000 may get the 2006 buyer onto the driver's seat of a Model 435. It will all depend on the tractor's special characteristics and who's there to buy. At a collectors' auction in June 2005, one 435 sold for more than $15,000.

Model 440

The Model 440 was an industrial series of tractors and crawlers introduced in January 1958. It was patterned after the Model 420 tractors. Based on the popularity of the Model 420 series, management at Deere believed an entirely new series of industrial-purpose machines would be big sellers.

From the start, the 440 had industrial styling. It had stronger sheet metal, better radiator protection, and a front-mounted hydraulic pump. For safety, the radiator and fuel caps were located under the hood, and the air cleaner was located behind the engine. Like the slant-dash 420 and 430, it had a slanted instrument panel and comfortable seat.

The final drive housing on Model 420C crawlers had been breaking too often. Deere responded with a much stronger casting on the 440. Hydraulic power could be used to tighten the 440's track. The four-roller option was dropped and all 440s were made with five rollers.

The 440 was introduced with the same two-cylinder engine used in the 420. In 1959, about halfway through the run, the engine was upgraded. It received a new, higher-compression cylinder head. With a boost to 2,000 rpm on the governor, the engine generated 10 percent more power.

The GM 2-53 diesel engine, the same as used in Model 435, was an option in 1959 and 1960. A little more than half of the 440s sold in this period had the GM diesel engine.

An innovation offered to crawler operators at the time was called Pilot Touch. A single lever could control both steering and reversing. It was a popular option to order, but it didn't work well. Most crawlers with the Pilot Touch were converted back to the original controls.

Other options included a rear PTO, belt pulley attachment, power steering, and Direction Reverser. The 440 could be used with a front-end loader, backhoes, rear blade, street sweeper, scarifier, snowplow, and three-point hitch implements.

These industrial crawlers and tractors are not a hot item in the collector's market at this time. About a dozen sales are recorded since 1999, nearly all for well under $5,000. The highest value by far was recorded in 2004 for a 1958 440I tractor. It sold for $9,000.

Production and Ratings

Model	Variant	Fuel	Model Years	Number Produced	Stars
H	"	All-Fuel	1938–1947	57,450	*
H	N	All-Fuel	1939–1947	978	***
H	NH	All-Fuel	1941–1947	37	*****
H	WH	All-Fuel	1941–1947	126	****
M	"	Gas	1947–1952	45,800	*
MC	"	Gas	1947–1952	10,510	*
MI	"	Gas	1947–1952	1,033	**
MT	"	Gas	1947–1952	30,473	*
40	T	Gas	1953–1955	17,433	*
40	T	All-Fuel	1953–1955	473	***
40	S	Gas	1953–1955	11,161	*
40	S	All-Fuel	1953–1955	653	***
40	C	Gas	1953–1955	11,407	*
40	C	All-Fuel	1953–1955	282	***
40	U	Gas	1954–1955	5,067	**
40	U	All-Fuel	1954–1955	141	****
40	W	Gas	1955	1,698	**
40	W	All-Fuel	1955	60	*****
40	V	Gas	1955	326	***
40	V	All-Fuel	1955	3	*****
40	H	Gas	1955	259	***
40	H	All-Fuel	1955	35	*****
320	S	Gas	1956–1958	1,836	**
320	S	All-Fuel	1956–1958	12	*****
320	S Slant-Steer	Gas	1956–1958	317	****
320	S Slant-Steer	All-Fuel	1956–1958	2	*****
320	U	Gas	1956–1958	716	***
320	U	All-Fuel	1956–1958	2	*****
320	U Slant-Steer	Gas	1956–1958	199	***
320	V	Gas	1956–1958	60–70	*****
420	S	Gas	1956–1958	3,806	**
420	S	LP	1956–1958	23	*****
420	S	All-Fuel	1956–1958	69	*****
420	U	Gas	1956–1958	4,872	**
420	U	LP	1956–1958	6	*****
420	U	All-Fuel	1956–1958	54	*****
420	W	Gas	1956–1958	11,197	*
420	W	LP	1956–1958	100	****
420	W	All-Fuel	1956–1958	399	***
420	H	Gas	1956–1958	559	***
420	H	LP	1956–1958	4	*****
420	H	All-Fuel	1956–1958	47	*****

Model		Fuel	Years	Number	Rarity
420	V	Gas	1956–1958	83	*****
420	V	All-Fuel	1956–1958	3	*****
420	T	Gas	1956–1958	7,580	**
420	T	LP	1956–1958	225	***
420	T	All-Fuel	1956–1958	234	***
420	I	Gas	1956–1958	255	***
420	C	Gas	1956–1958	17,644	*
420	C	LP	1956–1958	4	*****
420	C	All-Fuel	1956–1958	234	***
330	S	Gas	1958–1960	844	***
330	U	Gas	1958–1960	247	***
430	S	Gas	1958–1960	1,786	**
430	S	All-Fuel	1958–1960	18	*****
430	S	LP	1958–1960	5	*****
430	U	Gas	1958–1960	1,340	**
430	U	LP	1958–1960	10	*****
430	U	All-Fuel	1958–1960	3	*****
430	W	Gas	1958–1960	5,825	**
430	W	LP	1958–1960	88	*****
430	W	All-Fuel	1958–1960	68	*****
430	H	Gas	1958–1960	183	***
430	H	LP	1958–1960	27	*****
430	H	All-Fuel	1958–1960	63	*****
430	V	Gas	1958–1960	63	*****
430	T	Gas	1958–1960	3,103	**
430	T	All-Fuel	1958–1960	33	*****
430	T	LP	1958–1960	128	****
430	C	Gas	1958–1960	2,250	**
430	C	All-Fuel	1958–1960	33	*****
430	C	LP	1958–1960	4	*****
435	-	Diesel	1959–1960	4,488	**
440	I	Diesel	1958–1960	971	***
440	I	Gas	1958–1960	2,341	**
440	IC	Gas	1958–1960	9,855	*
440	IC	Diesel	1958–1960	6,679	*

Specifications

Model	H	M	40S	320/330S	420/430S	435
Width (in)	79	51	55.5	53.5	55.5	85.75
Height to radiator (in)	52	56	56	55.5	55.5	71.5
Length (in)	111.25	110	114.75	115.75	114.75	136.12
Weight (in)	2,063	2,560	2,750	2,750	2,750	3,750
Front tires/wheels (in)	4x15	4x15	5x15	5x15	5x15	5x15
Rear tires/wheels (in)	8x32	8x24	9x24	9x24	9x24	10-34
Fuel capacity (gal)	7.5	10	10.5	10.5	10.5	10.5
Coolant capacity (qt)	5.5	3.5	3.5	3.5	2.75	2.5

Gears forward/reverse *5th gear optional	3/1	4/1	4/1	4/1	4/1*	4/1

Engine / Power Data

	H	M	40S	420W	420C	435	440
Fuel	Dist.	Gas	Gas	Gas	Gas	Diesel	Gas
Nebraska Test No.	312	387	504	599	601	716	718
Nebraska Test year	10/31/38	10/6/47	9/9/53	10/13/56	10/15/56	9/8/59	9/10/59
Rated rpm	1,400	1,650	1,850	1,850	1,850	1,850	2,000
Bore and stroke (in)	3.56x5	4x4	4x4	4.25x4	4.25x4	3.87x4.5	4.25x4
Belt/PTO horsepower	14.84	20.45	24.9	29.21	29.72	32.91	31.06
Drawbar horsepower	12.48	18.15	22.4	27.08	24.12	28.41	26.9
Maximum pull	1,839	2,329	2,543	3,790	4,862	4,241	3,950
Shipping weight (lb)	3,035	3,952	4,189	5,781	5,079	6,057	5,975

Parts Prices

MODEL	H Low	H High	M Low	M High	40 Low	40 High	320 Low	320 High	420 Low	420 High	330 Low	330 High	430 Low	430 High	435 Low	435 High	440 Low	440 High
Air cleaner assembly	40		25		25		25		25		25		25					
Air cleaner intake stack																		
Amp gauge	22	70	28	50	25	50	28	50	28	50	20	50	28	50	28	50	28	
Battery box/cover	50	85	230	275	230	275	230	275	230	275	215	287	215	287				
Battery cable (set)	36		21		21													
Block	250																	
Camshaft	30	140	25	157	157		157		157				157					
Carburetor	175	533	147	377	147	377	147	377	147	377	147	377	147	377			147	377
Carburetor float	32	50	19	34	19	34	19	34	19	34	19	34	19	34			19	34
Carburetor kit	16	30	18	30	15	30	18	30	19	30	22		19	22			22	
Clutch drive disc	25		25															
Clutch pulley cover	20	33																
Clutch slider disc			109				109		109		109		109					
Connecting rod	60	156	25	70	60	66			60	66			60					
Crankshaft	45	145	50	351	378				525				525					
Cylinder head	200	335	320	394	320		320		369	375	320		369	375			369	375
Dash	20		30	50	50													
Distributor			169	205	169	205	169	205	145	205	169		145	205			145	205
Distributor cap			17		17		17		17		17		17				17	
Drag links																		
Engine overhaul kit	296		268		268		268				268							
Exhaust manifold	299		109	133	109	133	109	133	109	133	109	133	109	133			139	
Exhaust pipe	35	110	27	94	90	94	27	94	27	126	27	126	27	126	27	126	27	126
Fan assembly			65	109	89	109	65	109	89		100	109						
Fender	375	398	120		103	150	103	150	103	150	103	150	103	150	103	150		
Flywheel	40		60															
Flywheel cover	95	105																
Fuel tank	150		15		15													
Generator	120	179	120	179	120	179	120	179	120	179	120	179	120	179			120	179
Grille screen	15	60	17	52	35	87	39	55	35	87	39	55	35	87	65	69	49	
Grille with screen	185	225																

MODEL	H		M		40		320		420		330		430		435		440	
	Low	High	Low	High	Low	High	Low	High	Low	High	Low	High	Low	High	Low	High	Low	High
Headlight assembly	35	67	37	47	37	47	37	47	37	47	45		45					
Magneto	249	375																
Manifold (intake & exhaust)	210	275	80	133	100	133	100	133	100	133	100	133	108	135			133	135
Muffler	94		24	29	24	29	15	39	15	46	15	46	15	46	27	43	15	46
Overhaul kit (piston, rings, etc.)	210	325	275	428	275	427	275	427	290	425	275	427	290	425			290	425
Pan seat	35	55																
Piston	35								125				125				125	
Piston rings	79		69	72	69	72	69	72	75		69	72	75				75	
PTO shield	75	85	140	165	100	160	100	160	72	160	100	160	72	160	100	160		
Radiator			254	400	254	400	254	400	254	400	254	400	254	400				
Radiator cap	19	28	20	35	20	35	20	35	13	35	20	35	13	35	13	22	13	15
Radiator core	60	209	386	407	386	407	386	407	422		386	407	422					
Seat cushion (bottom)			26	45	26	45	26	45	26	45	26	45	26	45	26	45	26	45
Sediment bowl	45		24	28	24	28	24	28	24	28	24	28	24	28			24	28
Spark plug wires (set)	13	16	11	13	11	13	13		11	13	13		11	13	13		11	13
Starter	165	215	110	229	110	229	110	229	110	229	110	229	110	229	225	273	11	273
Starter drive assembly			30		30	46	30		30		30		30				30	
Steering wheel	44	90	44	52	44	65	52	125	52	125	52	125	52	125	52	125		
Three-point hitch			250	335														
Toolbox	25	37																
Voltage regulator			35	52	35	52	35	52	35	52	35	52	35	52			35	52
Water pump					120	190	120	190	120	190	120	190	75	190	149		120	190
Weight, front																		
Wheel bearings			29	51	29	51												
Wheel weights (405-lb set)																		

Ratings

Collector's 5-Star Editions LP Fuel

420S	23
420U	6
420H	4
420C	4
430S	5
430U	10
430H	27
430C	4

Collector's 5-Star Editions All-Fuel

HNH	37
40V	3
40H	35
320S	12
320S-SS	2
320U	2
420H	47
420V	3
430S	18
430U	3
430T	33
430C	33

Average Sale Value 1995 to 2010 (Actual and Projected)

Model H: *1939-1947*

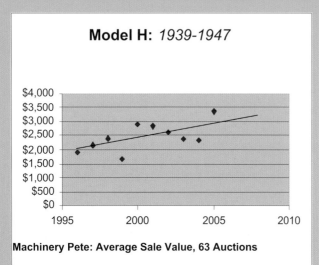

Machinery Pete: Average Sale Value, 63 Auctions

Model M: *1947-1952*

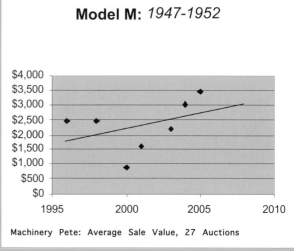

Machinery Pete: Average Sale Value, 27 Auctions

Model MT: *1949-1952*

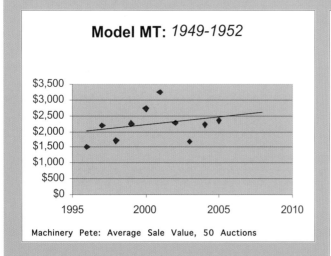

Machinery Pete: Average Sale Value, 50 Auctions

Model 40: *1953-1956*

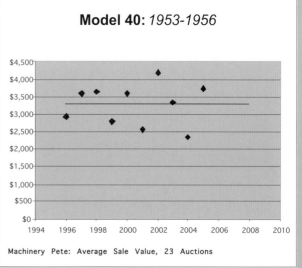

Machinery Pete: Average Sale Value, 23 Auctions

Average Sale Value 1995 to 2010 (Actual and Projected)

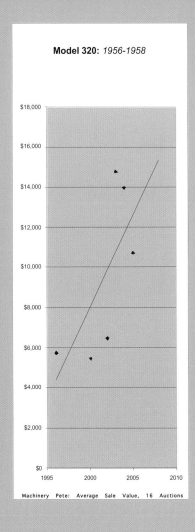

Model 320: *1956-1958*

Machinery Pete: Average Sale Value, 16 Auctions

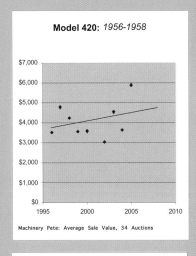

Model 420: *1956-1958*

Machinery Pete: Average Sale Value, 34 Auctions

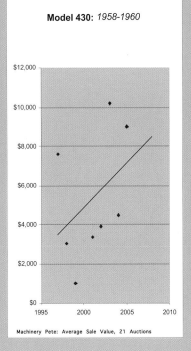

Model 430: *1958-1960*

Machinery Pete: Average Sale Value, 21 Auctions

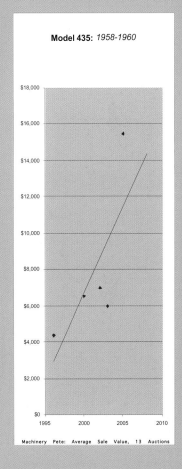

Model 435: *1958-1960*

Machinery Pete: Average Sale Value, 13 Auctions

Model 62. *Ron Jungmeyer*

Chapter 7

Models 62, L, LA

In the 1930s, every farm had a garden; most were large gardens for large families. Tens of thousands of farms had 5 to 20 acres of garden produce, which was enough to supply themselves and local markets. In the fields, tractors replaced horses in fields. A horse or a mule or a team pulled the garden implements. Deere managers decided that a tractor suited to the size of Depression-era farm market gardens could be a popular item when the economy recovered. It could be modeled after the very successful Model B, but would need to be much smaller and priced at around $500. Deere's smallest two-cylinder tractor for a garden emerged at a few retail dealerships in 1937.

At this point all Deere tractors were built at Waterloo. However, the development task for Deere's smallest tractor went to Ira Maxon, chief engineer at the John Deere Wagon Works plant in Moline. It would be easier to add in the tooling and assembly work there than to scale up further at Waterloo. In 1936, the Wagon Works team hand-built 24 experimental Model Y tractors and produced some sales literature. According to the literature, the one-plow Model Y weighed 1,340 pounds. It had a foot clutch instead of a hand clutch. This feature stayed with the series that followed in 1937.

The Model Y showed good potential for those big gardens and did pretty well in field tests, but needed improvement. Deere recalled all 24 Model Y tractors to the factory and built them into a better garden tractor with a new name and new sales literature. These emerged in 1937 with a whole line of appropriate implements for gardening as the Model 62. The Model Y ceased to exist, although at least one replica has been built just to show what it looked like.

Rather than build its own smaller engine for this tractor, Deere tried adapting an existing engine from another manufacturer.

Its first attempt for the Model Y was a new two-cylinder vertical engine, the Novo C-66. This engine was intended for stationary use. It had barely enough power to move the little tractor and didn't have enough oil capacity for work on hillsides. The second attempt was a two-cylinder built by Hercules, a company that specialized in small-engine development. This Hercules NXA generated an adequate 10 horsepower with a 3x4-inch bore and stroke. The Novo came out and the NXA went into the recalled Model Y tractors that winter. In addition, Moline workers began hand-building more units of the Model 62 in March 1937.

The assembly-line production of Deere's smallest tractor began at Moline in August 1937. One major assembly line at Moline was devoted to the family of little tractors for the next eight years. The last, an industrial LI, was shipped on April 5, 1946, to Omaha.

As a family, these were the only tractors built at Moline by John Deere. For Deere, they were the first tractor to have a vertical two-cylinder engine and the first tractor to have a foot clutch. They included the first Numbered tractor, and this tractor, the 62, was the only 100th anniversary tractor for Deere & Co.

Model 62

Deere's smallest and largest tractors were new products in 1937. That spring Deere began building the new 4,400-pound 1938 Model G at Waterloo; it was introduced later in the year. In January, the first of 78 tractors was readied at Moline for introduction as the 1,515-pound 1937 Model 62. It was a prototype to the Model L. The Model 62 tractors are rare, but most do still exist. They've been the pet project for Steve Ridenour and sons, Dale and Dwayne, of Trenton, Ohio. The

The cast JD logo on the front and rear is a distinguishing feature of the Model 62. *Dale Ridenour*

The Model 62 carried the Hercules NXA engine. The engine was offset left of center and mounted forward on a dual frame. The driver's seat, steering wheel, and shaft were offset to the right. *Dale Ridenour*

This is the only known Model 62 that was factory equipped for dual rear wheels. The Model 62 introduced features like a gasoline-only engine, a foot-operated clutch, and individual rear wheel brakes. *Dale Ridenour*

family has owned a few, restored a few, organized events for them, and has listed more than 60 models now in private collections.

Rebuilt from the Y, the Model 62 was mostly a new tractor. It was only 91 inches long, 49 inches wide, and 60 inches tall. The origin of its designation is uncertain. Most related production records were destroyed for both the 62 and the early L that followed. The Model 62 kept the Hercules NXA engine hooked to a Spicer transmission and rear end, but it was very different from the Y. It had new sheet metal, including

two-piece fenders. The front carried a large casting of the JD logo below the radiator. This casting helped make the front end stronger and gave mounting points for the engine. A second cast logo was on the rear differential. The serial number plate was located on the rear axle housing.

The Hercules engine had been mounted on the later Model Y with a slight tilt. On the 62, it was level. The Ford Model A automotive transmission first tested in the Y was replaced in Model 62 tractors with the Spicer, a three-speed

A Model 62 and an unstyled L are fender-to-fender to show some of the changes introduced for the L series. *Bruce Keller*

transaxle that had the transmission and differential as one unit. This allowed a belt pulley, driven by the driveshaft, to be fitted as an option.

"A lot of these 62s were almost built from the ground up to get them back to being a tractor," says Steve Ridenour. Since 2000, at least three or four Model 62 tractors have been discovered by collectors, and more may yet be found. The Model 62 and later Moline tractors are small enough that even an urban hobbyist can work on restoring one in the car garage. Ridenour has had some original parts and has had others reproduced so the tractors can be rebuilt. Reproduction parts that are now available include the radiator, driveline cover, sheet metal, wheel rims, cast centers for the rear wheels, and JD logo castings for the front. The only parts you really can't reproduce are the bell housing, transmission, clutch housing, engine, and frame.

The range in value in the 2006 market for these tractors is between $35,000 and $50,000, depending on condition.

Model 62 Buyers' Guide

"We've got two 62s yet in our collection that we will not get rid of. One has a set of rear dual wheels that are specifically 62 and there's no knowledge of another set in existence anyplace. That tractor will stay here. The other tractor [belonged to] the dealer in Michigan that gave John Deere the concept of building a small tractor like the L. John Deere took his information and worked on it, and this is the first tractor he got for sale after they actually built the 62. We've got newspaper articles from 1937 showing that this was the tractor. That won't go anywhere, either.

"I'm having a picture of a 62 engraved on my gravestone. I went to a funeral a while back for a guy that was heavy into steam trains. They had a beautiful picture engraved on that monument with a steam locomotive. I told the boys before I die I want to see what my gravestone will look like with the 62. That's how crazy we get into stuff sometimes."

— Steve Ridenour, Trenton, Ohio

An early unstyled Model L closely resembled the Model 62 without the big cast logo. *Ron Jungmeyer*

This is one of the first Model L tractors built in 1939 with the Dreyfuss styling treatment. Unstyled earlier models had the John Deere logo below the radiator. *Ron Jungmeyer*

The styled Model LI, an industrial tractor, had a lower seat and wider wheel tread than the Model L. *Jacob Merriwether*

Model L Unstyled

The Deere Wagon Works was ready to go into full-scale production with its new $500 market garden tractor after the summer break in 1937. It would handle cultivating 5 to 20 acres very nicely. It was time for a new name that would bring Moline's littlest tractor in line with the other Letter series tractors from Waterloo. Thus, the Moline assembly line built its first Model L tractor in August 1937. Workers put out 1,500 of these tractors before the annual shutdown in 1938.

Literature promoted the Model L as a light, economical tractor that could handle all the work normally done by one team of horses. It had 7 horsepower on the drawbar and was built to pull an implement. It didn't have a PTO or hydraulic power to lift an implement, but it could pull a single 12-inch plow in second gear in most situations. Instead of heavy casting, the tractor's basic framework was comprised of steel tubing. The engine and steering were offset to make it easy for the operator to see the rows. Deere provided a line of implements for the Model L, too. There were breakaway shovels, regular shovels, V-shaped shovels, and spring-type shovels. There were special metal shields for cultivating near certain vegetables. Other equipment options included a belt pulley for running a hammer mill and a mower that was useful for a small hayfield.

This is a 1944 Model LA in Illinois. It has noticeably larger and heavier rear wheels than the Model L. *Robert Kennell*

This styled Model LA is equipped with a 540-rpm PTO and a belt pulley. It has cast center rear wheels instead of the steel disk wheels found on the Model L. *Ron Jungmeyer*

Deere developed its own 10-horsepower gas engine for Model L tractors that could be attached to an electric starter and generator. The engine is rated for 1,850 rpm. *Dale Ridenour*

This Deere engine had a one-piece casting for the block and clutch housing but no provision for an oil filter. Spark plugs are four fingers apart, compared to only two fingers on the NXA engine. *Dale Ridenour*

The Model L had a foot clutch and dual brake pedals. With individual rear brakes it could turn in a 7-foot circle. *Dale Ridenour*

At first glance, the Model L and Model 62 were nearly identical. On the Model L, the big JD logo casting wasn't needed. The rear fenders were now one piece and a little smaller. This saved a little on production cost and gained an option to fit a mounted sickle bar mower to the little tractor. The rear wheel casting was replaced by a steel disk with five slots.

The Hercules NXA vertical two-cylinder engine was standard for this 1937 and 1938 Model L series. Meanwhile, Deere developed its own gasoline engine for the little tractor family. The Deere engine had a one-piece casting for the block and clutch housing. It also made a provision for a starter and generator.

The Model L had a three-speed automotive-style transmission and kept the foot clutch. With individual rear brakes, it could turn in a 7-foot circle. Vegetable and row-crop growers liked the adjustable rear tread.

For the first time on a John Deere two-cylinder tractor, rubber tires were standard and not optional. Electric starting was optional.

The Model L and its successors had problems with front-end spindles and the drag links had a tendency to wear out. The engine was vulnerable to premature wear. It did not have an oil filter. If the air cleaner was plugged, the engine could suck in dirt and wear out the rings.

Collectors are looking for these Model L tractors, and the supply is good but not large. Most of the 1,500 Model L tractors went into the region from New York west to Pennsylvania, Indiana, Ohio, and Michigan. In recent years a few have been

With a $36 starter and generator plus a $7 lighting package, this little 1944 tractor was easy to start year-round and set for driving home after dark. *Dale Ridenour*

exported to Europe, Australia, and New Zealand. Twenty-five years ago, these little tractors could be purchased for their original price, which was about $500. Today's average unstyled Model L in good shape and with most of the original parts may sell for $5,000; a very nice unrestored Model L that's ready for loving restoration may command as much as $10,000 in a private sale.

Model L Styled

Moline began building a styled L tractor in August 1938. The styled L went through some changes, but stayed on the production line until July 1946. It was a little more powerful and proved to be very popular. Nearly 11,000 of these were sold.

Styled L tractors initially had 10 horsepower thanks to a ¼-inch increase in the cylinder bore in the NXB Hercules engine. After about 4,000 of these were built, Deere started putting in its own transmission to replace the Spicer. The Deere transmission shift lever sits to the right, rather than on top. In July 1941, Deere replaced the Hercules engine. The Deere engine had the same bore and stroke as the Hercules and produced the same power. It had the same piston rods, same valves, valve springs, and timing gear. But a generator and electric starter could be attached to this engine. The clutch housing was cast onto the engine rather than bolted. Spark plugs on the Deere engine were four fingers apart rather than two, and it had a separate set of parts numbers.

Along with the styled L in 1938, Deere introduced the LI, an industrial version. These were usually painted industrial yellow or orange. They had shorter front spindles and rear-wheel spacers that gave it a shorter, wider stance. More important, the LI had the first hydraulics in the L family. With hydraulic power, these tractors could operate a No. 7 sickle mower. Less than 2,500 were manufactured.

Late in production, electric lights and an electric starter were available as an option. A PTO was never offered, but an optional belt pulley was available.

Auction records indicate steadily increasing values for the unstyled and styled L over the past 10 years. A rule of thumb: If it was worth $2,500 in 1996, it's worth $5,000 in 2006.

Model L Buyers' Guide

"We've got an original 1939 styled L that, to this day, has never been overhauled. We bought it off a farmer who was the second owner. He'd bought it when it was two years old and maintained it meticulously. He was 77 years old when we bought it. He used it to cultivate corn and he had several accessories. All we did was put a paint job on it. It doesn't burn oil or nothing."

— Steve Ridenour, Trenton, Ohio

Model LA

Two major changes occurred for the Model L family in 1941. One was the introduction of the new engine for Models L/LI. The second was the introduction of a new and bigger member, the Model LA, with an even bigger engine. The LA had 40 percent more power, weighed a third more, and had a bit more crop clearance. It weighed in at 2,200 pounds, compared to 1,550 pounds for the Model L. The Model LA had a solid-bar frame, rather than tubular steel, and stood 2 inches taller on cast rear wheels.

To gain more power, the LA engine bore was increased to 3.5 inches and the engine speed was bumped from 300 to 1,850 rpm. The revised engine kicked out 13 horsepower on the drawbar and 14 horsepower on the belt.

Model 62 Ancedote

"There's so many stories that connect to the 62 that it's not funny. Our first one is probably unique. Eaton, Ohio, is only 25 miles north of us. In 1987, we caught a rumor that there was one at Eaton, so we started hunting and we found it. The owner had just a little house, not a farm, and he had this 62 in his garage. He used it to go across the road and into the woods to get firewood. A four-cylinder Continental motor was in it when he bought it. He'd found it in a subdivision in Dayton a number of years before that. It was sitting along the road, for sale. He bought that thing for little or nothing. We told him that if he ever wanted to sell it we would be interested. A year or two later, his widow found our business card and sent us a newspaper clipping where it would be sold. We went and bought that 62 in 1987. We brought it back and we were fortunate enough to find the correct engine. The tubes were extended, so we cut them off and were able to put the tractor back to totally original. We sold that tractor three years ago to a gentleman in the East. We didn't want to sell it, but we had other fish to fry at the time. We haven't had a lot of money to work with this, and the hobby has to support itself."

— Steve Ridenour, Trenton, Ohio

Options included an electric starter and generator ($36), lighting ($7), adjustable front axle ($11), a 540-rpm PTO ($30), wheel weights ($7), and a belt pulley ($19).

Moline built about 12,500 LAs over the next five years. The basic model price was $560, only $65 more than the little brother.

Collectors have tuned in more to the LA than to the L in the past decade. Both are worth about the same today, but the LA market value has risen faster over the decade. In 1996, it was about $500 less than the Model L.

Model LA Buyers' Guide

"I don't believe in selling serial number plates, but I know people that do. A lot of times, serial number plates are missing off of tractors. On your little L and LA, they were on the rear axle housing and over half the tractors you find don't have a serial number on them. You can sell a serial number for $500." – Malcolm McIntyre, White House, Tennessee

"They're a very well-built tractor. They're overbuilt, really. There's way more driveline than you have engine. With normal use, I don't think anything behind the clutch would ever wear out. Just regular maintenance [is needed]. They're roughly the same size as a cub Farmall, but they're built a lot heavier." – Ron Jungmeyer, Jungmeyer Tractor Restoration Service, Russellville, Missouri

The basic Model L rear drawbar was mounted to the tubular main frame. Options included a PTO, belt pulley, or mud lug wheels.
Dale Ridenour

A porthole provides access to the starter and electrical connections. Electric starting was new and optional when this tractor was built.

Dale Ridenour

Production and Ratings

Model	Variant	Fuel	Model Years	Number Produced	Stars
Y	Unstyled	Gas	1936	24	N/A
62	Unstyled	Gas	1937	72	*****
L	Unstyled	Gas	1938	1,502	***
L	Styled	Gas	1939-1946	10,946	*
LI	Styled	Gas	1939-1946	2,452	**
LA	Styled	Gas	1941-1946	12,475	*

Specifications

Model	62/L/LI	LA
Width (in)	49	47
Height to radiator (in)	57	60
Length (in)	91	93
Weight (lb)	1,515	2,200
Front tires/wheels (in)	4x15	5x15
Rear tires/wheels (in)	6x22	8x24
Fuel capacity (gal)	6	8
Coolant capacity (qt)	2.5	2.5
Gears forward/reverse	3/1	3/1

Engine / Power Data

Fuel	Gas	Gas
Nebraska Test No.	313	373
Nebraska Test year	11/4/38	6/20/41
Rated rpm	1,550	1,850
Bore and stroke (in)	3.25x4	3.5x4
Belt/PTO horsepower	10.42	14.34
Drawbar horsepower	9.06	13.10
Maximum pull	1,235	1,936
Shipping weight (lb)	2180	3490

Parts Replacement
Parts Prices

Model	L Low	High	LA Low	High
Air cleaner assembly	120	135	120	135
Air cleaner intake stack				
Amp gauge			20	28
Battery box/cover	65		65	
Battery cable (set)			24	
Block	250		250	
Camshaft	120		25	120
Carburetor	147	375	147	320
Carburetor float	13		13	

Model	L		LA	
	Low	High	Low	High
Carburetor kit	15	22	15	22
Clutch drive disc				
Clutch pulley cover				
Clutch slider disc				
Connecting rod	110	150	20	113
Crankshaft			20	
Cylinder head				
Dash				
Distributor				
Distributor cap				
Drag links	40		40	
Engine overhaul kit	229			
Exhaust manifold	135			
Exhaust pipe	68			
Fan assembly	75		75	
Fender				
Flywheel				
Flywheel cover	10		10	
Fuel tank			45	
Generator	100	179	100	179
Grille screen				
Grille with screen				
Headlight assembly	37	45	37	45
Magneto	150	249	150	375
Manifold (intake & exhaust)	120	180	150	
Muffler	100		56	100
Overhaul kit (piston, rings, etc.)	249	255		
Pan seat	35	75	40	75
Piston	45		60	
Piston rings	72		72	
PTO shield			60	75
Radiator				
Radiator cap	15		15	
Radiator core				
Seat cushion (bottom)				
Sediment bowl				
Spark plug wires (set)	13	17	13	17
Starter	145	229	145	229
Starter drive assembly	30		30	
Steering wheel	44	65	44	65
Three-point hitch				
Toolbox				
Voltage regulator				
Water pump				
Weight, front				
Wheel bearings				
Wheel weights (405-lb set)				

Average Sale Value 1995 to 2010 (Actual and Projected)

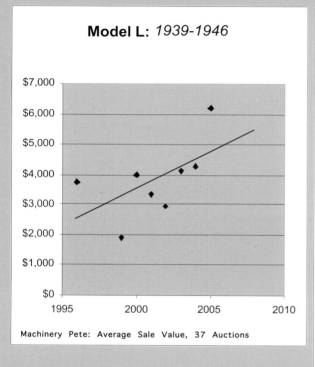

Model L: *1939-1946*

Machinery Pete: Average Sale Value, 37 Auctions

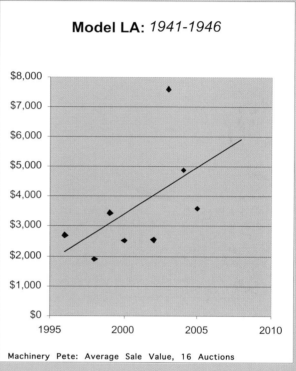

Model LA: *1941-1946*

Machinery Pete: Average Sale Value, 16 Auctions

Notes

1 *The John Deere Unstyled Letter Series*, *Green Magazine* 2000, by J. R. Hobbs, p. 23.

2 Ibid., p. 31.

3 "Here's why they didn't call it an AS or an A standard. The decision was first made to call it a Model AS. At a later meeting, the big wheels said we're going to come out with a Model B one of these days! You know what fun the competition would have had with that 'BS' model name? So they changed it to R for regular." — Ron Jungmeyer, Missouri

4 *The John Deere Unstyled Letter Series*, by J. R. Hobbs, p. 76.

5 *The John Deere Unstyled Letter Series*, J. R. Hobbs, p. 85.

6 *The John Deere Styled Letter Series*, J. R. Hobbs, *Green Magazine*, 2002, pp. 64-65

7 *The John Deere Styled Letter Series*, 2002, Hain Publishing Co., p. 79.

8 Malcolm McIntyre, Tennessee.

Buyer's Checklist (Developed by Howard Miller, Friend, Nebraska)

MODEL_____ YEAR_____ SERIAL #_____

CONDITION

3-Point _____Yes_____   No_____

Fenders _____Yes_____   No_____

Front Weights ____Yes_____   No_____

Rear Weights ____Yes_____   No_____

Air Stack _____Yes_____   No_____

Power Steering __Yes_____   No_____

P.T.O. Shield ____Yes_____   No_____

Step _____Yes_____   No_____

New Paint _____Yes_____   No_____

CONDITION

Hood _____

Nose Cone _____

Steering Wheel _____

Muffler _____

Seat _____

Cushions _____

Battery Box _____

Manifold _____

Radiator _____

Rims _____

Tires Rear _____   Size _____

Tires Front _____   Size _____

Brakes _____

Clutch _____

Gauges _____

Tachometer _____   Hr. Meter Reading _____

Drawbar _____

P.T.O. _____

Transmission _____

Engine _____

Front End: Tricycle _____   Single _____   W.F. _____

Comments: _____

_____

_____

Index

Look for these additional books from Voyageur Press

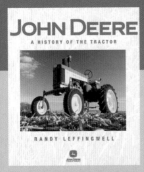
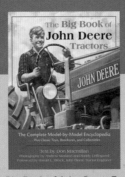
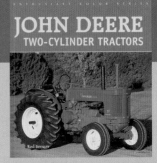
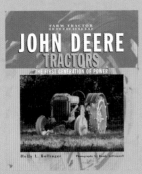
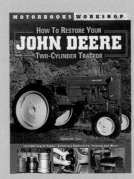
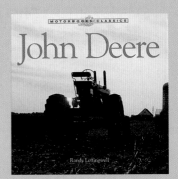

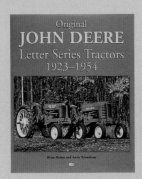
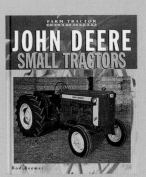